MW00812871

CONTENTS

for pattern inquiries, please visit www.knitsimplemag.com
or www.go-crafty.com

STRIPED tee

You'll Need

YARN (4)

- 8¾oz/250g (8¾/250g, 10½oz/300g, 12¼oz/350g, 12¼oz/350g, 14oz/400g) or 460yd/430m (460yd/430m, 560yd/510m, 650yd/600m, 650yd/600m, 740yd/680m) of any worsted weight cotton in taupe (A)
- 5¼oz/150g (5¼oz/150g, 7oz/200g, 7oz/200g, 8¾/250g, 8¾/250g or 280yd/260m (280yd/260m, 370yd/340m, 370yd/340m, 460yd/430m, 460yd/430m) in light blue (B)
- 1¾oz/50g (1¾oz/50g, 1¾oz/50g, 3½oz/100g, 3½oz/100g, 3½oz/100g) or 100yd/90m (100yd/90m, 100yd/90m, 190yd/170m, 190yd/170m, 190yd/170m) in lime green (C) and yellow (D)

NEEDLES

- Size 9 (5.5mm) circular needle, 24"/61cm long *or size to obtain gauge*
- One size 8 (5mm) circular needle, 16"/40cm long
- One pair size 8 (5mm) knitting needles

OTHER MATERIALS

- Stitch marker

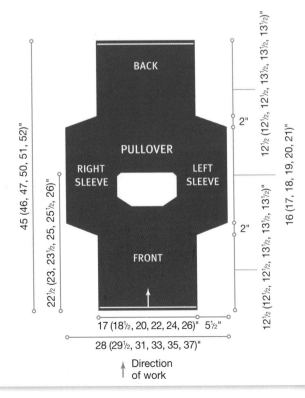

SIZES

Sized for Small, Medium, Large, 1X, 2X, 3X. Shown in size Medium.

KNITTED MEASUREMENTS

Bust 34 (37, 40, 44, 48, 52)"/86.5 (94, 101.5, 111.5, 122, 132) cm
Length 22½ (23, 23½, 25, 25½, 26)"/57 (58.5, 59.5, 63.5, 64.5, 66) cm
Upper arm 20 (21, 22, 23, 24, 25)"/51 (53.5, 56, 58.5, 61, 63.5 cm

GAUGE

18 sts and 24 rows to 4"/10cm over St st using larger circular needle. (**Note** To ensure a good fit and stripes that match from front to back, be sure to get the row gauge as well as the stitch gauge.)
Take time to check gauge.

NOTES

1 Pullover is made in one piece from front to back.
2 Body of sweater is worked back and forth; circular needle is used to accommodate large number of sts.

STITCH GLOSSARY

Stripe Pattern
Working in St st, work *6 rows B, 4 rows C, 6 rows B, 4 rows D; rep from * (20 rows) for stripe pat.

TEE

Beg at front bottom edge, with straight needles and A, cast on 78 (84, 90, 100, 108, 118) sts. Work in garter st for 4 rows. Change to larger circular needles. Working back and forth, work in St st for 16 (16, 16, 22, 22, 22) rows. Rep stripe pat twice, then work first 16 rows once (56 rows). Change to A.

Shape front sleeves
Cast on 4 sts at beg of next 12 rows—126 (132, 138, 148, 156, 166) sts. Work even for 2 (6, 8, 12, 14, 18) rows. Rep stripe pat once, then work 6 rows B. AT THE SAME TIME, when 4 rows of 2nd B stripe has been completed, work as foll:

Shape front neck
Next row (RS) K 52 (55, 58, 63, 67, 72) sts, join a 2nd ball of B and bind off center 22 sts, k to end. Keeping to stripe pat each side, bind off 5 sts at each neck edge once, then 3 sts once, end with a WS row.
Dec row (RS) With first ball of yarn, k to last 3 sts, k2tog; with 2nd ball of yarn, k1, ssk, k to end. Purl next row.

Rose Callahan

Rep last 2 rows twice more—41 (44, 47, 52, 56, 61) sts each side. When stripe pat is completed, change to A. Work even for 20 rows.

Shape back neck
Inc row (RS) With first ball of yarn, k to last st, M1, k1; with 2nd ball of yarn, k1, M1, k to end. Purl next row. Rep last 2 rows once more—43 (46, 49, 54, 58, 63) sts each side. Cut 2nd ball of yarn.

Next row (RS) With first ball of yarn, k to last st, cast on 40 sts, with first ball of yarn, k to end—126 (132, 138, 148, 156, 166) sts. Work even for 15 rows, end with a WS row. Reverse stripe pat as foll: Work 6 rows B, 4 rows D, 6 rows B, 4 rows C and 6 rows B. Change to A. Work even for 2 (6, 8, 12, 14, 18) rows.

Shape back sleeves
Bind off 4 sts at beg of next 12 rows—78 (84, 90, 100, 108, 118) sts. Rep stripe pat twice, then work first 16 rows once (56 rows). Change to A and work for 16 (16, 16, 22, 22, 22) rows. Change to straight needles. Work in garter st for 5 rows. Bind off all sts knitwise.

FINISHING
Block piece to measurements.

Neck edging
With RS facing, smaller circular needle and A, beg at center back neck and pick up and k 132 sts evenly spaced around neck edge. Join and pm for beg of rnds. Work around in garter st for 4 rnds. Bind off all sts purlwise.

Sleeve edging
With RS facing, straight needles and A, pick up and k 72 (76, 80, 86, 90, 94) sts evenly spaced along armhole edge. Work in garter st for 3 rows. Bind off all sts purlwise. Sew side and sleeve seams.

PLEAT neck top

You'll Need

YARN (4)

- 14oz/400g (15¾oz/450g, 17½oz/500g, 21oz/600g, 22¾oz/650g) or 760yd/700 (860yd/790m, 950yd/870m, 1140yd/1050m, 1240yd/1140m) of any worsted weight cotton blend

NEEDLES

- Size 6 (4mm) circular needle, 29"/73cm *or size to obtain gauge*
- Three size 6 (4mm) double-pointed needles (dpns) for pleats

OTHER MATERIALS

- Stitch markers

SIZES

Sized for Small, Medium, Large, 1X, 2X. Shown in size Small.

KNITTED MEASUREMENTS

Bust 35 (38, 41, 44, 48)"/89 (96.5, 104, 111.5, 122)cm
Length 21 (21½, 22½, 23½,24)"/53.5 (54.5, 57, 59.5, 61)cm
Upper arm 11½ (12½, 13½, 14½, 15½)"/29 (31.5, 34, 37, 39.5)cm

GAUGE

20 sts and 28 rows to 4"/10cm over St st using size 6 (4mm) circular needle.
Take time to check gauge.

STITCH GLOSSARY

12-st LP (left pleat) Sl next 4 sts to dpn #1, sl next 4 sts to dpn #2, sl next 4 sts to dpn #3. Hold dpn #1 in front so RS is facing, bring dpn #2 to back so WS is tog with WS of dpn #1. Bring dpn #3 to back so RS is tog with RS of dpn #2. [K 1 st from each dpn tog] 4 times.

12-st RP (right pleat) Sl next 4 sts to dpn #1, sl next 4 sts to dpn #2, sl next 4 sts to dpn #3. Hold dpn #1 in so RS is facing, bring dpn #2 to front so RS is tog with RS of dpn #1. Bring dpn #3 to front so WS is tog with WS of dpn #2. [K 1 st from each dpn tog] 4 times.

Seed stitch (multiple of 2 sts)
Rnd 1 (RS) *K1, p1; rep from * around.
Rnd 2 Knit the p sts and purl the k sts.
Rep rnd 2 for seed st.

BODY

Cast on 174 (190, 204, 220, 240) sts. Join and pm for beg of rnds.
Work around in seed st for 4 (4, 4, 6, 6) rnds.
Next rnd K 87 (95, 102, 110, 120) sts, pm, k to end. Cont on St st until piece measures 2 (2, 2½, 3, 3)"/5 (5, 6.5, 7.5, 7.5)cm from beg.

Shape sides

Next (dec) rnd K1, k2tog, k to 3 sts before next marker, ssk, k1, sl marker, k1, k2tog, k to 3 sts before next marker, ssk, k1.
Rep dec rnd every 7th rnd 3 times more—158 (174, 188, 204, 224) sts. Work even until piece measures 7 (7, 7½, 8, 8)"/17.5 (17.5, 19, 20.5, 20.5)cm from beg.
Next (inc) rnd K1, M1, k to 1 st before next marker, M1, k1, sl marker, k1, M1, k to 1 st before next marker, M1, k1.
Rep inc rnd every 11th rnd 3 times more—174 (190, 204, 220, 240) sts. Work even until piece measures 14 (14, 14½, 15, 15)"/35.5 (35.5, 37, 38, 38)cm from beg, end 8 (9, 10, 11, 12) sts before beg of rnd marker.

Shape armholes

Next rnd Bind off next 16 (18, 20, 22, 24) sts dropping marker, k to 8 (9, 10, 11, 12) sts before next marker, bind off next 16 (18, 20, 22, 24) sts dropping marker, k to end.

YOKE

Shape sleeves

Next rnd Pm, cast on 57 (61, 67, 73, 77) sts, pm, k 71 (77, 82, 88, 96) sts, pm, cast on 57 (61, 67, 73, 77) sts, pm, k to end—256 (276, 298, 322, 346) sts.
Next rnd P1, *k1, p1; rep from * to next marker, k to next marker, p1, *k1, p1, rep from * to next marker, k to end.
Next rnd K1, *p1, k1; rep from * to next marker, k to next marker, k1, *p1, k1; rep from * to next marker, k to end. Rep last 2 rnds 1 (1, 1, 2, 2) times more.

For Small size only
Work even in St st on 256 sts for 31 rnds.

For Medium size only
Work even in St st on 276 sts for 22 rnds.
Dec rnd *K7, k2tog, [k13, k2tog] 3 times, k7, sl marker, k5, k2tog, [k11, k2tog] 5 times, k5, sl marker; rep from * once more—256 sts. Work even for 11 rnds.

For Large size only
Work even in St st on 298 sts for 13 rnds.
Dec rnd 1 *K to next marker, k5, k2tog, [k12, k2tog] 5 times, k5, sl marker; rep from * once more—286 sts.
Work even for 12 rnds.
Dec rnd 2 *K7, k2tog, [k15, k2tog] 3 times, k7, sl marker, k7, k2tog, [k8, k2tog] 6 times, k7, sl marker; rep from * once more—264 sts. Work even for 11 rnds.

For 1X size only
Work even in St st on 322 sts for 14 rnds.
Dec rnd 1 *K6, k2tog, [k13, k2tog] 4 times, k5, sl marker, k7, k2tog, [k16, k2tog] 4 times, k7, sl marker; rep from * once more—302 sts. Work even for 13 rnds.
Dec rnd 2 *K5, k2tog, [k12, k2tog] 4 times, k5, sl marker, k5, k2tog, [k12,

k2tog] 5 times, k6, sl marker; rep from * once more—280 sts. Work even for 11 rnds.

For 2X size only
Work even in St st on 346 sts for 11 rnds.

Dec rnd 1 *K9, k2tog, [k17, k2tog] 3 times, k9, sl marker, k7, k2tog, [k14, k2tog] 5 times, k7, sl marker; rep from * once more—326 sts. Work even for 10 rnds.

Dec rnd 2 *K6, k2tog, [k13, k2tog] 4 times, k5, sl marker, k7, k2tog, [k13, k2tog] 5 times, k6, sl marker; rep from * once more—304 sts. Work even for 10 rnds.

Dec rnd 3 *K5, k2tog, [k12, k2tog] 4 times, k5, sl marker, k5, k2tog, [k10, k2tog] 6 times, k5, sl marker; rep from * once more—280 sts. Work even for 10 rnds.

For all sizes
As you work pleat rnd, drop all markers. The last pleat will be worked a few sts into the following rnd.

For Small and Medium sizes only
Next (pleat) rnd K9, [k8, 12-st LP, 12-st RP] 8 times, pm for beg of rnd—128 sts.

For Large size only
Next (pleat) rnd K8, [k9, 12-st LP, 12-st RP] 8 times, pm for beg of rnd—136 sts.

For 1X and 2X sizes only
Next (pleat) rnd K10, [k10, 12-st LP, 12-st RP] 8 times, pm for beg of rnd—152 sts.

For all sizes

Neckband
Work around in seed st for 5 (5, 5, 7, 7) rnds. Bind off in seed st.

FINISHING
Block piece to measurements.

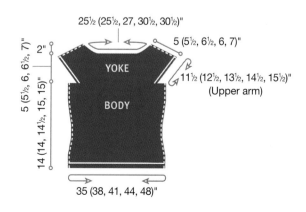

25½ (25½, 27, 30½, 30½)"

5 (5½, 6½, 6, 7)"

2"

YOKE

BODY

5 (5½, 6, 6½, 7)"

14 (14, 14½, 15, 15)"

11½ (12½, 13½, 14½, 15½)"
(Upper arm)

35 (38, 41, 44, 48)"

BROKEN rib top

You'll Need

YARN

- 10½oz/300g (12¼oz/350g, 12¼oz/350g, 14oz/400g, 15¾oz/450g, 17½oz/500g, 17½oz/500g) or 920yd/840m (1080yd/980m, 1080yd/980m, 1230yd/1120m, 1300yd/1260m, 1530yd/1400m, 1530yd/1400m) of any DK weight wool blend

NEEDLES

- One pair and one circular size 6 (4mm) needles *or size to obtain gauge*

OTHER MATERIALS

- Stitch holder or safety pin
- Stitch markers

SIZES

Sized for X-Small, Small, Medium, Large, X-Large, 2X, 3X. Shown in size Medium.

KNITTED MEASUREMENTS

Bust 44 (48, 52, 56, 60, 64, 68)"/111.5 (122, 132, 142, 152, 162.5, 172.5)cm
Length 22½ (23½, 24, 24½, 25, 26, 26½)"/57 (60, 61, 62, 63.5, 66, 67.5)cm

GAUGE

22 sts and 32 rows to 4"/10cm over garter ridge pat (slightly stretched and blocked) using size 6 (4mm) needles. Take time to check gauge.

STITCH GLOSSARY

Rib pat (multiple of 3 sts)
Row 1 (RS) K1, *p1, k2; rep from *, end p1, k1.
Row 2 K2, *p2, k1; rep from *, end k2.
Rep rows 1 and 2 for rib pat.

Garter ridge pat (multiple of 3 sts)
Rows 1 and 3 (RS) K1, *p1, k2; rep from *, end p1, k1.
Row 2 K2, *p2, k1; rep from *, end k2.
Row 4 Knit.
Rep rows 1-4 for garter ridge pat.

BACK

Cast on 120 (132, 144, 156, 165, 177, 186) sts. Work in rib pat for 1½"/4cm. Cont in garter ridge pat until piece measures 13 (13½, 13½, 14, 14, 14½, 14½)"/33 (34.5, 34.5, 35.5, 35.5, 37, 37)cm from beg.

Armhole detail

Next row (RS) K1, [p1, k2] twice, p1, cont garter ridge pat to last 8 sts, [p1, k2] twice, p1, k1. Cont in this way to work first and last 8 sts in rib pat and rem sts in garter ridge pat, until piece measures 21½ (22½, 23, 23½, 24, 25, 25½)"/54.5 (57.5, 58.5, 59.5, 61, 63.5, 65)cm from beg

Shape shoulder

Bind off 8 (10, 11, 12, 13, 15, 16) sts at beg of next 4 rows, 9 (10, 11, 13, 14, 15, 16) sts at beg of next 4 rows. Bind off rem 52 (52, 56, 56, 57, 57, 58) sts knitwise for back neck.

FRONT

Work as for back until piece measures 15 (15½, 16, 16½, 16½, 17½, 18)"/38 (39.5, 40.5, 42, 42, 44.5, 45.5)cm from beg.

Shape V-neck

Next row (RS) Work 58 (64, 70, 76, 80, 86, 91) sts, k2tog (neck dec), join a 2nd ball of yarn and for sizes X-Large and 2X only, bind off center st, for all sizes, work rem sts as foll: SKP (neck dec), work to end. Working both sides at once, work as foll: Work 1 row even. Cont in this way to dec 1 st at each neck edge every other row 25 (25, 27, 27, 27, 27, 28) times more, AT THE SAME TIME, when piece measures 21½ (22½, 23, 23½, 24, 25, 25½)"/54.5 (57.5, 58.5, 59.5, 61, 63.5, 65)cm from beg, bind off from each shoulder edge 8 (10, 11, 12, 13, 15, 16) sts twice, 9 (10, 11, 13, 14, 15, 16) sts twice.

FINISHING

Block pieces to measurements, or keep unblocked for a more fitted look. Sew shoulder seams. Sew side seams to armhole ribbing.
Sew side seams to armhole ribbing.

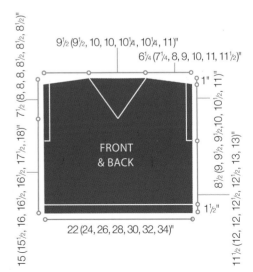

9½ (9½, 10, 10, 10¼, 10¼, 11)"
6¼ (7¼, 8, 9, 10, 11, 11½)"
1"
7½ (8, 8, 8, 8½, 8½, 8½)"
8½ (9, 9½, 9½, 10, 10½, 11)"
FRONT & BACK
11½ (12, 12, 12½, 12½, 13, 13)"
1½"
22 (24, 26, 28, 30, 32, 34)"
15 (15½, 16, 16½, 16½, 17½, 18)"

Rose Callahan

CLASSIC top

You'll Need

YARN (3)

- 10½oz/300g(10½oz/300g, 12¼oz/350g, 14oz/400g, 15¾oz/450g, 19¼oz/550g) or 1050yd/960m (1050yd/960m, 1230yd/1120m, 1400yd/1280m, 1580yd/1440, 1930yd/1760m) of any DK weight cotton blend

NEEDLES

- One pair each sizes 6 and 7 (4 and 4.5mm) needles *or size to obtain gauge*

OTHER MATERIALS

- Stitch markers

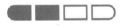

SIZES

Sized for Small, Medium, Large, 1X, 2X, 3X. Shown in size Medium.

KNITTED MEASUREMENTS

Bust 34 (36, 38, 42, 46, 50)"/86 (91.5, 96.5, 106.5, 117, 127)cm
Length 22½(23, 23½, 24, 24½, 25)"/57 (58.5, 59.5, 61,62, 63.5)cm
Upper arm 11½ (12, 13, 15, 16, 17)"/29 (30.5, 33, 38, 40.5, 43)cm

GAUGE

20 sts and 28 rows to 4"/10cm over St st using size larger needles.
Take time to check gauge.

NOTE

Lower edges of body and sleeves are knitted on after main pieces are complete.

BACK

With larger needles, cast on 85 (90, 95, 105, 115, 125) sts. Work in St st for 12"/30.5cm.

Shape armhole
Bind off 3 (3, 3, 4, 5, 6) sts at beg of next 2 rows, then 2 sts at beg of next 2 (2, 2, 4, 4, 6) rows.
Dec row 1 (RS) Knit to last 4 sts, SKP, k2.
Dec row 2 (WS) Purl to last 4 sts, p2tog, p2.
Rep the last 2 rows 5 (6, 7, 7, 9, 9) times more—63 (66, 69, 73, 77, 81) sts. Work even until armhole measures 7½ (8, 8½, 9, 9½, 10)"/19 (20.5, 21.5, 23, 24, 25.5) cm.

Shape shoulder
Bind off 3 (3, 4, 4, 5, 5) sts at beg of next 4 rows, 3 (4, 3, 5, 4, 6) sts at beg of next 2 rows. Bind off rem 45 (46, 47, 47, 49, 49) sts for back neck.

FRONT

Work as for back until armhole measures 3½ (4, 4½, 5, 5½, 6)"/9 (10, 11.5, 12.5, 14, 15)cm. On the last WS row, place markers to mark the center 15 (16, 17, 17, 19, 19) sts.

Shape neck
Next row (RS) K to the center marked sts, join a 2nd ball of yarn and bind off center 15 (16, 17, 17, 19, 19) sts, k to end. Cont to work each side with separate balls of yarn, bind off 3 sts from each neck edge once then 2 sts once. Then dec 1 st at each neck edge every RS row 10 times—9 (10, 11, 13, 14, 16) sts rem each side. Work even until armhole measures same as back.

Shape shoulder
Bind off 3 (3, 4, 4, 5, 5) sts from each shoulder edge twice, then 3 (4, 3, 5, 4, 6) sts once.

SLEEVES

With larger needles, cast on 50 (52, 57, 61, 66, 71) sts. Work in St st, inc 1 st each side every 8th (8th, 8th, 4th, 4th, 4th) row 4 (4, 4, 7, 7, 7) times—58 (60, 65, 75, 80, 85) sts. Work even until piece measures 6"/15cm from beg.

Shape cap
Bind off 3 (3, 3, 4, 5, 6) sts at beg of next 2 rows, then 2 sts at beg of next 2 (2, 2, 4, 4, 4) rows.
Dec row 1 (RS) Knit to last 4 sts, SKP, k2.
Dec row 2 (WS) Purl to last 4 sts, p2tog, p2.
Rep [dec rows 1 and 2] 9 (10, 12, 14, 16, 17) times more. Work 2 rows even. Rep dec rows 1 and 2. Rep the last 4 rows once more. Bind off 2 sts at beg of next 4 rows. Bind off rem 16 (16, 17, 17, 16, 17) sts.

Sleeve bands
With smaller needles, cast on 6 sts.
Row 1 (RS) K to the last st, sl last st, insert LH needle into cast-on st at edge of sleeve and k this loop, place this st and slipped st back on LH needle and k these sts tog, turn.
Row 2 (WS) Sl 1 wyif, p to the last st, sl 1 wyif. Rep rows 1 and 2 until band fits along the cast-on edge of the sleeve.

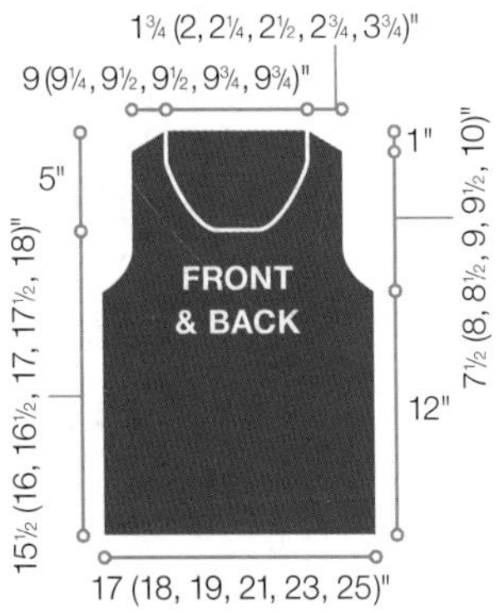
1¾ (2, 2¼, 2½, 2¾, 3¾)"
9 (9¼, 9½, 9½, 9¾, 9¾)"
5"
1"
FRONT
& BACK
15½ (16, 16½, 17, 17½, 18)"
7½ (8, 8½, 9, 9½, 10)"
12"
17 (18, 19, 21, 23, 25)"

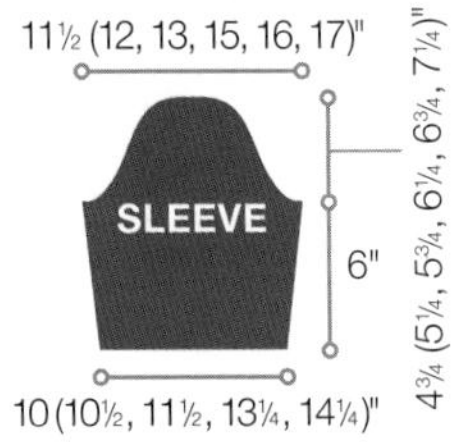
11½ (12, 13, 15, 16, 17)"
SLEEVE
6"
4¾ (5¼, 5¾, 6¼, 6¾, 7¼)"
10 (10½, 11½, 13¼, 14¼)"

Bind off. Sew shoulder seams. Set in sleeves. Sew side and sleeve seams.

Lower band
With smaller needles, cast on 9 sts, Work as for sleeve bands to fit entire lower edge of body. Bind off. Sew the band tog at the seam.

COLLAR
With smaller needles, cast on 4 sts.
Row 1 (WS) Purl.
Row 2 (RS) Cast on 2 sts, k to end.
Row 3 and all WS rows Sl 1 wyif, purl to end.
Rows 4 and 6 Rep row 2.
Row 8 Inc 1 st, knit to end.
Rows 10, 12, 14 and 16 Rep row 8—15 sts.
Cont in St st (always sl 1 wyif at beg of WS rows) until piece measures approx 33½ (34, 34½, 34½, 35, 35)"/85 (86, 87.5, 87.5, 89, 89)cm from beg.
Next row (RS) SKP, k to end.
Next row Sl 1 wyif, purl to end. Rep [the last 2 rows] 11 times more. Bind off. Place marker to mark center back neck and pin center collar at this marker. Sew collar to neck beg at the right shaped neck and around the back neck, then for the remainder of the collar that fits around the front, pin so that collar will "drape down" by approx 1¼"/3cm from the neck edge and sew in place. (This is so that the under collar will be shown as in the photo).

Rose Callahan

DEEP V tunic

You'll Need

YARN (4)

- 10½oz/300g(12¼oz/350g, 14oz/400g, 15¾oz/450g, 17½oz/500g) or 540yd/500m (630yd/580m, 720yd/660m, 810yd/740m, 900yd/820m) of any worsted weight cotton

NEEDLES

- One pair size 9 (5.5mm) needles *or size to obtain gauge*
- Size 9 (5.5mm) circular needle, 29"/73cm long

OTHER MATERIALS

- Stitch holders and stitch markers

SIZES

Sized for Small, Medium, Large, 1X, 2X. Shown in size Small.

KNITTED MEASUREMENTS

Bust 34 (38, 42, 45½, 49½)"/86.5 (96.5, 106.5, 115.5, 125.5)cm
Length 25 (25½, 26, 26½, 27)"/63.5 (64.5, 66, 67.5, 68.5)cm
Upper arm 11 (12, 13, 14, 15)"/28 (30.5, 33, 35.5, 38)cm

GAUGE

17 sts and 26 rows to 4"/10cm over St st using size 9 (5.5mm) needles.
Take time to check gauge.

STITCH GLOSSARY

Kf&b Inc 1 by knitting into the front and back of the next st.

3-needle bind-off
1 With RS tog, hold pieces on two parallel needles. Insert 3rd needle knitwise into first st of each needle and wrap yarn around each needle as if to knit.
2 Knit these 2 sts tog and sl them off the needles. *K the next 2 sts tog in the same manner.
3 Sl first st on 3rd needle over the 2nd st and off the needle. Rep from * in step 2 across row until all sts are bound off.

Border rib pattern
(multiple of 8 sts plus 3)
Row 1 (RS) K3, *p2, k1, p2, k3; rep from * to end.
Row 2 K1, p1, k1, *k6, p1, k1; rep from * to end.
Rep rows 1 and 2 for border rib.

BACK

Cast on 75 (83, 91, 99, 107) sts. Work in border rib for 5½"/14cm, end with a WS row. Cont in St st and work even for 1"/2.5cm, end with a WS row.

Shape sides
Next (dec) row (RS) K1, ssk, k to last 3 sts, k2tog, k1. Work next 3 rows even. Rep last 4 rows 6 times more—61 (69, 77, 85, 93) sts. Work even until piece measures 11½"/29cm from beg, end with a WS row.
Next (inc) row (RS) K1, kf&b, k to last 2 sts, kf&b, k1. Work next 5 rows even. Rep last 6 rows 5 times more—73 (81, 89, 97, 105) sts. Work even until piece measures 17½"/44.5cm from beg, end with a WS row.

Shape cap sleeves
Next (inc) row (RS) K2, kf&b, k to last 3 sts, kf&b, k2. Purl next row. Rep last 2 rows 7 times more—89 (97, 105, 113, 121) sts. Mark beg and end of last row for beg of armholes.
Next row (RS) Sl 1 wyib, k to end.
Next row Sl 1 wyif, p to end. Rep last 2 rows until armhole measures 4½ (5, 5½, 6, 6½)"/11.5 (12.5, 14, 15, 16.5)cm, end with a WS row.

Shape Neck
Next row (RS) Sl 1 wyib, k 27 (31, 35, 39, 43), join a 2nd ball of yarn and bind off center 33 sts, k to end. Working both sides at once, cont as foll:
Next row (WS) With first ball of yarn, sl 1 wyif, p to end; with 2nd ball of yarn, p to end.
Next (dec) row (RS) With first ball of yarn, sl 1 wyib, k to last 3 sts, k2tog, k1; with 2nd ball of yarn, k1, ssk, k to end.
Next row (WS) With first ball of yarn, sl 1 wyif, p to end; with 2nd ball of yarn, p to end. Rep last 2 rows once more. Place rem 26 (30, 34, 38, 42) sts each side on holders. Armhole should measure 5½ (6, 6½, 7, 7½)"/14 (15, 16.5, 17.5, 19)cm above marked row.

FRONT

Work as for back, AT THE SAME TIME, when piece measures 13½ (13½, 14, 14, 14½)"/34 (34, 35.5, 35.5, 37)cm from beg, end with a WS row.

Shape Neck
Next row (RS) Work to center 3 sts, join a 2nd ball of yarn and bind off center 3 sts, work to end. Working both sides at once, work next row even.
Next (dec) row (RS) With first ball of yarn, work to last 3 sts, k2tog, k1; with 2nd ball of yarn, k1, ssk, work to end. Cont to dec 1 st from each neck edge every 4th row 13 times more; then every 6th row 3 times. When all shaping has been completed, work even on 26 (30,

Rose Callahan

3-needle bind-off. Rep for right shoulder.

Neckband

With RS facing and circular needle, beg at left shoulder seam and pick up and k 60 (62, 62, 64, 64) sts evenly spaced along left neck edge, pick up and k 1 st in first of 3 bound-off sts, place marker (pm), pick up and k 1 st in center st, pm, pick up and k 1 st in last st, pick up and k 60 (62, 62, 64, 64) sts evenly spaced along right neck edge to shoulder, then 45 sts along back neck edge to left shoulder—168 (172, 172, 176, 176) sts. Join and pm for beg of rnds.

Next rnd P to 2 sts before first marker, p2tog, sl marker, p1, sl marker, p2tog tbl, p to end.

Next rnd Bind off knitwise to 2 sts before first marker, ssk, drop marker, bind off to next marker, drop marker, k2tog, cont to bind off knitwise to end, dropping rnd marker.

Sew side and underarm seams.

34, 38, 42) sts each side until piece measures same length as back to shoulders, end with a WS row. Place rem 26 (30, 34, 38, 42) sts each side on holders.

FINISHING

Block pieces to measurements. To join left shoulder, place 26 (30, 34, 38, 42) sts from left back holder on straight needle ready for a RS row, then place 26 (30, 34, 38, 42) sts from left front holder on straight needle ready for a RS row. With RS tog, hold pieces on two parallel needles. Cont to work

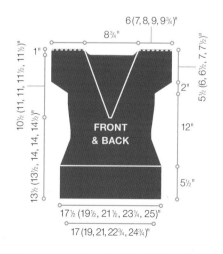

6 (7, 8, 9, 9¾)"

8¾"

1"

10½ (11, 11, 11½, 11½)"

2"

5½ (6, 6½, 7, 7½)"

12"

FRONT & BACK

13½ (13½, 14, 14, 14½)"

5½"

17½ (19½, 21½, 23¼, 25)"

17 (19, 21, 22¾, 24¾)"

TIE neck blouse

You'll Need

YARN [3]

- 14oz/400g (14oz/400g, 15¾oz/450g, 17½oz/500g, 19¼oz/550g) or 1080yd/990m (1080yd/990m, 1220yd/1110m, 1350yd/1230m, 1490yd/1360m) of any DK weight cotton blend

NEEDLES

- One pair each sizes 4 and 5 (3.5 and 3.75mm) needles *or size to obtain gauge*

OTHER MATERIALS

- Cable needle (cn)

SIZES

Sized for Small, Medium, Large, X-Large and XX-Large. Shown in size Small.

KNITTED MEASUREMENTS

Bust 34 (36½, 39, 48, 51)"/86.5 (92.5, 99, 122, 129.5)cm
Length 23 (23½, 24, 25¾, 26¾)"/58.5 (59.5, 61, 65.5, 68)cm
Upper arm 13¼ (14, 14¾, 16, 17)"/33.5 (35.5, 37.5, 40.5, 43) cm

GAUGE

22 sts and 30 rows to 4"/10cm over St st using larger needles.
Take time to check gauge.

BACK

With smaller needles, cast on 101 (109, 115, 139, 149) sts.
Row 1 (RS) P2 (selvage sts), k1, *p1, k1; rep from *, end p2 (selvage sts).
Rows 2-4 K the knit sts and p the purl sts. Change to larger needles.

Set-up pattern

Row 1 (RS) P2, k47 (51, 54, 66, 71), p1, k1, p1, k47 (51, 54, 66, 71), p2.
Row 2 K the knit sts and p the purl sts. Cont in pat as set-up for 8 rows more.
Center line dec row (RS) P2, k to 2 sts before the center 3 rib sts, k2tog, p1, k1, p1, ssk, k to last 2 sts, p2. Rep dec row every 10th row 5 times more—89 (97, 103, 127, 137) sts. Work even until piece measures 11"/28cm from beg.
Center line inc row (RS) Work to 2 sts before center 3 sts, inc 1 st in next st, k1, p1, k1, p1, inc 1 st in next st, work to end. Rep inc row every 8th row twice more—95 (103, 109, 133, 143) sts.
Work even until piece measures 15¼"/39cm from beg.

Shape armholes

Bind off 6 (6, 6, 8, 8) sts at beg of next 2 rows. Bind off 2 sts at beg of next 2 (4, 6, 8, 8) rows.
Dec row (RS) K1, SKP, work to the last 3 sts, k2tog, k1. Rep dec row every other row 4 (4, 4, 5, 6) times more—69 (73, 75, 89, 97) sts. Work even until armhole measures approx 2½ (3, 3½, 4½, 5)"/6.5 (7.5, 9, 11.5, 12.5) cm.
Rep center line inc row on next RS row, then every 8th row twice more—75 (79, 81, 95, 103) sts.
Work even until armhole measures 5½ (6, 6½, 7½, 8)"/14 (15, 16.5, 19, 20.5) cm, place markers to mark the center 29 (33, 35, 37, 41) sts on the last WS row.

Shape neck

K to center marked sts, join a 2nd ball of yarn and bind off these center 29 (33, 35, 37, 41) sts, k to end. Cont to shape neck binding off 3 sts from each neck edge 3 times AT SAME TIME, when armhole measures 6½ (7, 7½, 8½, 9)"/16.5 (18, 19, 21.5, 23) cm. Work shoulder shaping as foll:

Shape shoulders

Row 1 (RS) K2, SKP, k to end of first side; on 2nd side, k to the last 4 sts, k2tog, k2.

Row 2 (WS) P2, p2tog, p to end of first side; on 2nd side, p to the last 4 sts, p2tog tbl, p2.
Rep [rows 1 and 2] 4 (4, 4, 7, 8) times more. Then rep row 1 once more—3 sts rem each side. Bind off.

FRONT

Work as for back until piece measures 13¾ (14¼, 14¾, 15¼, 15¼)"/35 (36, 37.5, 39, 39) cm from beg.

Shape neck

Note The armhole shaping will beg with the neck shaping on the top 2 sizes only. For the other sizes, beg the armhole shaping when piece measures 15¼"/39cm from beg.
Next row (RS) K to center 21 (25, 27, 29, 33) sts, join a 2nd ball of yarn and bind off these sts, k to end. Working both sides at once, work even for 1 row.
Neck dec row (RS) Work to last 3 sts of first side, k2tog, k1; on 2nd side, k1, ssk, work to end. Rep neck dec row every 6th row 9 times more—14 (14, 14, 20, 22) sts rem each side. Work even until armhole measures 6½ (7, 7½, 8½, 9)"/16.5 (18, 19, 21.5, 23) cm.

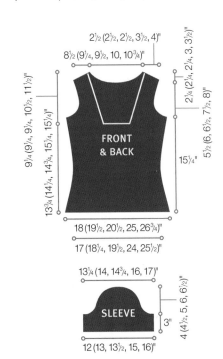

2½ (2½, 2½, 3½, 4)"

8½ (9¼, 9½, 10, 10¾)"

9¼ (9¼, 9¼, 10½, 11½)"

13¾ (14¼, 14¾, 15¼, 15¼)"

2¼ (2¼, 2¼, 3, 3½)"

5½ (6, 6½, 7½, 8)"

FRONT & BACK

15¼"

18 (19½, 20½, 25, 26¾)"

17 (18¼, 19½, 24, 25½)"

13¼ (14, 14¾, 16, 17)"

4 (4½, 5, 6, 6½)"

SLEEVE

3"

12 (13, 13½, 15, 16)"

Rose Callahan

Row 1 (WS) Purl.
Inc row 2 (RS) K1, inc 1 st in next st, k to end.
Rep [the last 2 rows] 8 times more. P1 row on RS for turning ridge.
Row 1 (WS) Purl.
Dec row 2 K2, ssk, k to end. Rep [the last 2 rows] 8 times more—50 (50, 50, 54, 59) sts. Bind off purlwise.

FINISHING

Sew other shoulder and collar seam. Fold collar in half to WS and sew in place. Sew the 2"/5cm seam of the collar along the opening (for tie to pull through). Set in sleeves. Sew side and sleeve seams.

TIE

First half
With smaller needles, cast on 37 sts.
Row 1 (RS) K18, sl 1 wyib, k18. **Row 2** Purl. Rep these 2 rows for a total of 24 rows.
Pleat row (RS) K2, sl 7 sts to cn and hold at back, [then k1 st from needle at front along with 1 st from cm at back] 7 times, k2, sl 1, k2, [k2tog] 7 times, k2—23 sts. Work even for 24 rows. Sl these sts to a holder.

Second half
Work as for first half up to the pleat row.
Pleat row (RS) K2, [k2tog] 7 times, k2, sl 1, k2, sl 7 sts to cn and hold at back, [then k1 st from needle at front along with 1 st from cn at back] 7 times, k2. Complete as for first half. Using 3-needle bind-off (refer to page 10), join the 2 halves tog at the center. Seam the sides and lower ends of the tie. Block lightly. Pull the tie through the opening and tack in place, if desired.

Shape shoulders
Work as for back.

SLEEVES

With smaller needles, cast on 67 (71, 75, 83, 87) sts. Work in k1, p1 rib for 4 rows. Change to larger needles and k next row, inc 1 st each side of row. Cont in St st, inc 1 st each side every 6th row twice more—73 (77, 81, 89, 93) sts. Work even until piece measures 3"/7.5cm from beg.

Shape cap
Bind off 6 sts at beg of next 2 rows, bind off 2 sts at beg of next 4 rows.
Dec row (RS) K1, SKP, k to the last 3 sts, k2tog, k1. Rep dec row every other row 7 (9, 11, 15, 17) times more. Bind off 2 sts at beg of next 4 rows, 3 sts at beg of next 2 rows, 4 sts at beg of next 2 rows. Bind off rem 15 sts.

COLLAR

Note The collar is worked in two parts,

with the back neck and left front edge worked first, then the right front edge worked afterwards.
Sew left shoulder seam. With smaller needles, pick up and k 65 (69, 71, 73, 77) sts across back neck, then 41 (41, 41, 45, 50) sts from left front neck—106 (110, 114, 118, 127) sts.
Row 1 (WS) Purl.
Inc row 2 K to the last 3 sts, inc 1 st in next st, k2. Rep [the last 2 rows] 8 times more—115 (119, 123, 127, 136) sts. P1 row on RS for turning ridge.
Row 1 (WS) Purl.
Dec row 2 (RS) K to the last 4 sts, k2tog, k2. Rep [the last 2 rows] 8 times more—106 (110, 114, 118, 127) sts. Bind off purlwise.

Right front edge
With smaller needles, cast on 10 sts, then skip approx 2"/5cm at the lower neck edge (for opening) and pick up and k 31 (31, 31, 35, 40) sts along this edge to the shoulder—41 (41, 41, 45, 50) sts.

TEXTURED V-neck

You'll Need

YARN 3

- 17½oz/500g (21oz/600g, 24½oz/700g, 28oz/800g, 31½oz/900g, 31½oz/900g) or 1030yd/940m (1230yd/1130m, 1440yd/1310m, 1640yd/1500m, 1850yd/1690m, 1850yd/1690m) of any DK weight cotton

NEEDLES

- One pair each sizes 5 and 6 (3.75 and 4mm) needles *or sizes to obtain gauge*

OTHER MATERIALS

- Stitch markers

SIZES

Sized for Small, Medium, Large, 1X, 2X, 3X. Shown in size Small.

KNITTED MEASUREMENTS

Bust 34 (38, 42, 47, 51, 53½)"/86.5 (96.5, 106.5, 119.5, 129.5, 136)cm
Length 21½ (22, 23, 24, 24½, 25)"/54.5 (56, 58.5, 61, 62, 63.5)cm
Upper arm 12 (13, 14, 15, 16, 17)"/30.5 (33, 35.5, 38, 40.5, 43)cm

GAUGES

22 sts and 28 rows to 4"/10cm over broken St st using larger needles.
21 sts and 36 rows to 4"/10cm over seed st using larger needles.
Take time to check gauges.

STITCH GLOSSARY

Broken Stockinette
(multiple of 6 sts plus 3)
Rows 1 and 5 (RS) Knit.
Row 2 and all WS rows Purl.
Row 3 K1, p1, k1, *k4, p1, k1; rep from * to end.

Row 7 K3, *k1, p1, k4; rep from * to end.
Row 8 Purl.
Work rows 1–8 for broken St st.

Seed stitch (multiple of 2 sts plus 1)
Row 1 (RS) P1, *k1, p1; rep from * to end.
Row 2 Knit the p sts and purl the k sts. Rep row 2 for seed st.

BACK

With smaller needles, cast on 93 (105, 117, 129, 141, 147) sts. Work in seed st for 4 rows, end with a WS row. Change to larger needles and broken St st. Work even until piece measures 2½ (2½, 3, 3½, 3½, 3½)"/6.5 (6.5, 7.5, 9, 9, 9)cm from beg, end with a WS row.

Shape waist

Next (dec) row (RS) K1, ssk, work to last 3 sts, k2tog, k1. Rep dec row every 6th row 5 times more.
Work even on 81 (93, 105, 117, 129, 135) sts until piece measures 7½ (7½, 8, 8½, 9, 9)"/19 (19, 20.5, 21.5, 23, 23)cm from beg, end with a WS row.
Next (inc) row (RS) K1, M1, work to last st, M1, k1. Rep inc row every 4th row 5 times more. Work even on 93 (105, 117, 129, 141, 147) sts until piece measures 13½ (13½, 14, 14½, 14½, 14½)"/34 (34, 35.5, 37, 37, 37)cm from beg, end with a WS row.

Shape armholes

Bind off 6 (7, 8, 9, 11, 11) sts at beg of next 2 rows. Dec 1 st each side on next row, then every other row 2 (4, 6, 9, 10, 11) times more. Work even on 75 (81, 87, 91, 97, 101) sts until armhole measures 6½ (7, 7½, 8, 8½, 9)"/16.5 (17.5, 19, 20.5, 21.5, 23)cm, end with a WS row.

Neckband

Next row (RS) Work in broken St st over first 12 (15, 17, 19, 21, 23) sts, pm, work in seed st over center 51 (51, 53, 53, 55, 55) sts, pm, work in broken St st to end. Keeping center sts in seed st and rem sts in broken St st, work even until armhole measures 7¼ (7¾, 8¼, 8¾, 9¼, 9¾)"/18.5 (19.5, 21, 22, 23.5, 24.5)

cm, end with a WS row.

Shape neck

Next row (RS) Work in broken St st over first 12 (15, 17, 19, 21, 23) sts, sl marker, work in seed st over next 5 sts, join a 2nd hank of yarn and bind off center 41 (41, 43, 43, 45, 45) sts, work in seed st to next marker, sl marker, work in broken St st to end.
Working both sides at once, work next row even.

Shape shoulders

Keeping 5 sts at neck edge in seed st, bind off 5 (6, 8, 8, 8, 10) sts at beg of next 2 rows, then 6 (7, 7, 8, 9, 9) sts at beg of next 4 rows.

FRONT

Work as for back until piece measures 13½ (13½, 14, 14½, 14½, 14½)"/34 (34, 35.5, 37, 37, 37)cm from beg, end with a WS row.

Shape armholes

Next row (RS) Bind off 6 (7, 8, 9, 11, 11) sts, work in broken St st until there are 35 (40, 45, 50, 54, 57) sts on RH needle,

3 (3½, 4, 4¼, 4¾, 5)"
7½ (7½, 7¾, 7¾, 8, 8)"
½"
5½ (5½, 6, 6½, 6½, 6½)"
16 (16½, 17, 17½, 18, 18½)"
FRONT & BACK
7½ (8, 8½, 9, 9½, 10)"
13½ (13½, 14, 14½, 14½)"
17 (19, 21, 23½, 25½, 26¾)"

12 (13, 14, 15, 16, 17)"
SLEEVE
4½ (4¾, 5, 5¼, 5½, 5¾)"
11 (11½, 11½, 12, 12½, 13)"
9 (9, 9½, 9½, 10, 10)"

pm, k11, pm, work in broken St st to end.
Next row Bind off 6 (7, 8, 9, 11, 11) sts, p to end.
Cont to shape armholes as for back. AT THE SAME TIME, when armhole measures 1½ (2, 2½, 2, 2½, 3)"/4 (5, 6.5, 5, 6.5, 7.5)cm, end with a WS row, shape neckband as foll:

Beg neckband
Next row (RS) Work to first st marker, sl marker, k5, p1, k5, sl marker, work to end.
Next row Work to first st marker, sl marker, p4, k1, p1, k1, p4, sl marker, work to end.
Next row (RS) Work to first st marker, sl marker, k3, [p1, k1] twice, p1, k3, sl marker, work to end.
Next row Work to first st marker, sl marker, p2, [k1, p1] 3 times, k1, p2, sl marker, work to end.
Next row (RS) Work to first st marker, sl marker, [k1, p1] 5 times, k1, sl marker, work to end. Rep last row once more, end with a WS row.

Shape v-neck
Next row (RS) Work to first st marker, sl marker, work in seed st over next 5 sts; join a 2nd hank of yarn, bind off center st, work in seed st over next 5 sts, sl marker, work to end. Working both sides at once, work next row even.
Next (dec) row (RS) Work to 2 sts before first marker, k2tog, sl marker, work in seed st over next 5 sts; with 2nd hank of yarn, work in seed st over next 5 sts, sl marker, ssk, work to end. Rep dec row every other row 19 (19, 20, 20, 21, 21) times more. Work even on 17 (20, 22, 24, 26, 28) sts each side until piece measures same length as back to shoulders, end with a WS row. Shape shoulders as for back.

SLEEVES
With larger needles, cast on 47 (47, 49, 49, 53, 53) sts. Work in seed st until piece measures 3 (3, 3, 2, 2, 2)"/7.5 (7.5, 7.5, 5, 5, 5)cm from beg, end with a WS row. Inc 1 st each side on next row, then every 4th row 0 (0, 0, 2, 3, 7)

times more, every 6th row 0 (6, 10, 12, 12, 10) times, every 8th row 3 (4, 1, 0, 0, 0) times, every 10th row 4 (0, 0, 0, 0, 0) times.
Work even on 63 (69, 73, 79, 85, 89) sts until piece measures 11 (11½, 11½, 12, 12½, 13)"/28 (29, 29, 30.5, 31.5, 33)cm from beg, end with a WS row.

Shape cap
Bind off 5 (6, 7, 9, 10, 10) sts at beg of next 2 rows. Dec 1 st each side on next row, then every other row 14 (15, 16, 17, 18, 19) times more, every 4th row twice.

Bind off 2 sts at beg of next 4 rows. Bind off rem 11 (13, 13, 13, 15, 17) sts.

FINISHING
Block pieces to measurements. Sew shoulder seams. Set in sleeves. Sew side and sleeve seams.

SUNSHINE tee

You'll Need

YARN [3]

- 7oz/200g (8¾oz/250g, 8¾oz/250g, 10½oz/300g, 12¼oz/350g, 12¼oz/350g) or 770yd/700m (960yd/880m, 960yd/880m, 1150yd/1050m, 1340yd/1230m, 1340yd/1230m) of any DK weight cotton in yellow (MC)

- 5¼oz/150g (5¼oz/150g, 7oz/200g, 7oz/200g, 8¾oz/250g, 8¾oz/250g) or 580yd/530m (580yd/530m, 770yd/700m, 770yd/700m, 960yd/880m, 960yd/880m) in white (CC)

NEEDLES

- One pair size 9 (5.5mm) needles *or size to obtain gauge*

OTHER MATERIALS

- Size I/9 (5.5mm) crochet hook
- 4 stitch markers, scrap yarn or stitch holders

SIZES
Sized for X-Small, Small, Medium, Large, 1X, 2X. Shown in size X-Small.

KNITTED MEASUREMENTS
Bust 34 (36, 38, 40, 46, 48)"/86 (92, 96.5, 101.5, 117, 122)cm
Length 22 (23, 24, 24½, 26½, 27)"/56 (58.5, 61, 62, 67, 68.5)cm
Upper arm 12 (13, 13½, 14½, 15¼, 16¼)"/30.5 (33, 34, 7, 39, 41)cm

GAUGE
17 sts and 24 rows to 4"/10cm over St st using 2 strands of yarn held tog and size 9 (5.5mm) needles.
Take time to check gauge.

NOTES
1 Work with 2 strands of yarn held tog throughout.
2 Shape the neck edges using the sloped bind-off method as foll: on the row preceding the sts to be bound off, sl the last st of row. Then on the bind-off row, pass the first st over the 2nd st, then bind off as usual.

BACK
With 1 strand each A and B held tog, cast on 68 (72, 77, 81, 94, 98) sts. Work even in St st for 18 rows.
Dec row (RS) K1, k2tog, k to the last 3 sts, SKP, k1. Rep dec row every 18th row once more—64 (68, 73, 77, 90, 94) sts. Work even until piece measures 10 (10, 10½, 10½, 11, 11)"/25.5 (25.5, 26.5, 26.5, 28, 28)cm from beg.
Inc row (RS) K2, inc 1 st in next st, k to last 3 sts, inc 1 st in next st, k2. Rep inc row every 6th row every 3 times more—72 (76, 81, 85, 98, 102) sts. Work even until piece measures 14 (14½, 15, 15, 16, 16)"/35.5 (37, 38, 38, 40.5, 40.5)cm from beg.

Shape armhole
Bind off 4 (4, 4, 5, 5, 5) sts at beg of next 2 rows, 2 sts at beg of next 2 (2, 2, 2, 4, 4) rows, 1 st at beg of next 8 (8, 10, 10, 14, 16) rows—52 (56, 59, 61, 66, 68) sts. Work even until armhole measures 2½ (3, 3½, 4, 5, 5½)"/6.5 (7.5, 9, 10, 12.5, 14)cm. Cut B and cont with 2 strands A only until armhole measures 7 (7½, 8, 8½, 9½, 10)"/18 (19, 20.5, 21.5, 24, 25.5)cm

Shape neck and shoulder
Bind off 5 (5, 5, 6, 6, 6) sts at beg of next 4 rows, 5 (6, 6, 5, 7, 7) sts at beg of next 2 rows, AT SAME TIME, using the sloped bind-off method, bind off center 10 (12, 15, 15, 16, 18) sts and working both sides at once, bind off 3 sts from each neck edge twice.

FRONT
Work as for back until armhole measures 3½ (4, 4½, 5, 6, 6½)"/9 (10, 11.5, 12.5, 15, 16.5)cm. There should be 6 rows in solid A color at this point.

Shape neck
Next row (RS) Work 21 (22, 22, 23, 25, 25) sts, join a 2nd 2 strands of A and bind off center 10 (12, 15, 15, 16, 18) sts, work to end. Using the sloped bind-off method, bind off 2 sts from each neck edge once, 1 st 4 times—15 (16, 16, 17, 19, 19) sts rem each side. Work even until same length as back armhole. Shape armhole as on back.

SLEEVES
With 1 strand each A and B held tog, cast on 51 (55, 58, 61, 65, 69) sts. Work in St st for 6 rows or 1"/2.5cm.

Shape cap
Bind off 4 (4, 4, 5, 5, 5) sts at beg of next 2 rows, 1 st at beg of next 16 (18, 20, 20, 20, 22) rows—27 (29, 30, 31, 35, 37) sts. Work even for 2 (4, 4, 6, 8, 8) rows.

Bind off 2 sts at beg of next 6 rows. Bind off rem 15 (17, 18, 19, 23, 25) sts.

FINISHING
Do not block pieces. Sew shoulder seams. Sew side and sleeve seams. Set in sleeves.

Chain stitch trim
The trim is worked using a crochet hook and 2 strands of B held tog on the WS of work at 1 st or 1 row from each edge as foll: beg at lower side seam, from the RS, bring yarn through from the WS and ch 1, then insert hook in between next 2 sts or rows and work 1 sl st, cont around working sl sts loosely on the lower sleeve cuff and neck edges.

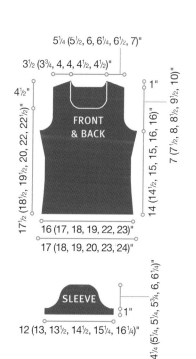

OPEN front pullover

You'll Need

YARN 4

- 14oz/400g (15¾oz/450g, 17½oz/500g, 19¼oz/550g) or 870yd/800m (980yd/900m, 1080yd/990m, 1190yd/1090m) of any worsted weight cotton yarn in blue (MC)
- 3½oz/100g (5¼/150g, 5¼/150g, 5¼/150g) or 220yd/200m (330yd/300m, 330yd/300m, 330yd/300m) in variegated blue-green (CC)

NEEDLES

- One pair size 7 (4.5mm) knitting needles *or size to obtain gauge*

OTHER MATERIALS

- Stitch holder

SIZES

Sized for X-Small, Small, Medium, Large. Shown in size X-Small.

KNITTED MEASUREMENTS

Bust 30 (33, 36, 38½)"/76 (84, 91.5, 97.5)cm
Length 23½ (24½, 25½, 26½)"/59.5 (62, 64.5, 67.5)cm
Upper arm 12½ (13, 13½, 14½)"/31.5 (33, 34, 37)cm

GAUGES

20 sts and 32 rows to 4"/10cm over seed st using size 7 (4.5mm) needles.
18 sts and 36 rows to 4"/10cm over garter st using size 7 (4.5mm) needles.
Take time to check gauges.

STITCH GLOSSARY

Seed stitch (multiple of 2 sts)
Row 1 *K1, p1; rep from * to end.
Row 2 Knit the p sts and purl the k sts.
Rep row 2 for seed st.

BACK

With MC, cast on 84 (92, 100, 106) sts. Work in seed st for 10 rows. Dec 1 st each side on next row, then every 10th row 4 times more—74 (82, 90, 96) sts. Work even until piece measures 8½"/21.5cm from beg, end with a RS row

Next (dec) row (WS) K across, dec 6 (6, 8, 10) sts evenly spaced—68 (76, 82, 86) sts. Change to CC and work even in garter st until piece measures 12½"/31.5cm from beg, end with a WS row. Change to MC.
Next (inc) row (RS) K across, inc 6 (6, 8, 10) sts evenly spaced—74 (82, 90, 96) sts. Cont in seed st and work even until piece measures 16½ (17, 17½, 18)"/42 (43, 44.5, 45.5)cm from beg, end with a WS row.

Shape armholes

Bind off 4 sts at beg of next 2 rows, then 2 sts at beg of next 2 rows. Dec 1 st each side every other row 3 times—56 (64, 72, 78) sts. Work even until armhole measures 6½ (7, 7½, 8)"/16.5 (17.5, 19, 20.5)cm, end with a WS row.

Shape neck and shoulders

Next row (RS) Work across first 20 (23, 27, 29) sts, join another ball of MC and bind off 16 (18, 18, 20) sts for back neck, work to end. Working both sides at once, bind off 5 sts each neck edge once, then 4 sts once, AT THE SAME TIME, bind off 6 (7, 9, 10) sts at each armhole edge once, then 5 (7, 9, 10) sts once.

FRONT

Lower left front

With MC, cast on 42 (46, 50, 53) sts. Work in seed st for 10 rows. Dec 1 st at beg of next RS row, then at same edge every 10th row 4 times more—37 (41, 45, 48) sts. Work even until piece

measures 8½"/21.5cm from beg, end with a RS row.

Lower right front

Work as for lower left front, reversing shaping, end with a RS row.

Join lower fronts

Next (dec) row (WS) K across lower right front sts, dec 3 (3, 4, 5) sts evenly spaced, then k across lower left front sts dec 3 (3, 4, 5) sts evenly spaced—68 (76, 82, 86) sts. Change to CC and work even in garter st until piece measures 12½"/31.5cm from beg, end with a WS row. Change to MC.
Next (inc) row (RS) K across, inc 6 (6, 8, 10) sts evenly spaced—74 (82, 90, 96) sts. Cont in seed st and work 1 row even.

Upper left front

Next row (RS) Work across first 37 (41, 45, 48) sts, place rem sts on holder

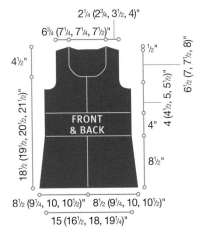

for upper right front. Work even until piece measures same length as back to armhole, end with a WS row. Shape armhole as for back—28 (32, 36, 39) sts. Work even until armhole measures 2 (2½, 3, 3½)"/5 (6.5, 7.5, 9)cm, end with a RS row.

Shape neck
Next row (WS) Bind off 8 (9, 9, 10) sts, work to end. Cont to bind off 4 sts from neck edge once, 2 sts once, then dec 1 st every other row 3 times—11 (14, 18, 20) sts. Work even until armhole measures same length as back to shoulder. Shape shoulder as for back.

Upper right front
Next row (RS) Place sts from holder back to LH needle. Cont to work as for upper left front, reversing all shaping.

SLEEVES
With CC, cast on 46 (48, 48, 50) sts. Work even in garter st until piece measures 4"/10cm from beg, end with a WS row. Change to MC. Cont in seed st and inc 1 st each side on next row, then every 8th row 7 (8, 9, 10) times more—62 (66, 68, 72) sts. Work even until piece measures 18 (18½, 19, 19½)"/45.5 (47, 48, 49.5)cm from beg, end with a WS row.

Shape cap
Bind off 4 sts at beg of next 2 rows, then 2 sts at beg of next 2 rows. Dec 1 st each side every other row 3 times—44 (48, 50, 54) sts. Work even until cap measures 4"/10cm, end with a WS row. Bind off 2 sts at beg of next 2 rows, 4 sts at beg of next 4 rows, then 6 sts at beg of next 2 rows. Bind off rem 12 (16, 18, 22) sts.

FINISHING
Lightly block pieces to measurements. Sew shoulder seams. Set in sleeves. Sew side and sleeve seams.

NickNorwood

LACY top

You'll Need

YARN ③

- 15¾oz/450g (17½oz/500g, 21oz/600g, 22¾oz/650g, 26¼oz/750g, 28oz/800g or 1080yd/990m (1200yd/1100, 1440yd/1320m, 1560yd/1430m, 1800yd/1650, 1920yd/1760m) skeins of any DK weight cotton blend

NEEDLES

- One pair size 8 (5mm) needles *or size to obtain gauge*
- Size 8 (5mm) circular needle, 16"/40cm long

OTHER MATERIALS

- Stitch markers, stitch holder or safety pin

SIZES

Sized for X-Small, Small, Medium/Large, X-Large, 2X, 3X. Shown in size Medium/Large.

KNITTED MEASUREMENTS

Bust 42 (47, 52½, 58, 63½, 68½)"/106.5 (119, 133, 147, 161, 174)cm
Length 22½ (23½, 24½, 25, 26, 26½)"/57 (60, 62, 63.5, 66, 67.5)cm

GAUGES

20 sts and 28 rows to 4"/10cm over St st using size 8 (5mm) needles.
18 sts and 28 rows to 4"/10cm over lace pat using size 8 (5mm) needles.
Take time to check gauges.

STITCH GLOSSARY

Lace pattern (multiple of 12 sts plus 1)
Note Work lace pat from written instructions below OR foll chart pat.
Row 1 (RS) *K1, yo, SKP, k7, k2tog, yo; rep from *, end k1.
Row 2 and all WS rows Purl.
Row 3 *K2, yo, SKP, k5, k2tog, yo, k1; rep from *, end k1.
Row 5 *K1, [yo, SKP] twice, k3, [k2tog, yo] twice; rep from *, end k1.
Row 7 *K2, [yo, SKP] twice, k1, [k2tog, yo] twice, k1; rep from *, end k1.
Row 9 *K3, yo, SKP, yo, SK2P, yo, k2tog, yo, k2; rep from *, end k1.
Row 11 *K4, yo, SKP, k1, k2tog, yo, k3; rep from *, end k1.
Row 13 *K5, yo, SK2P, yo, k4; rep from *, end k1.
Row 14 Purl.
Rep rows 1-14 for lace pat.

BACK

Cast on 99 (111, 125, 137, 151, 163) sts. Work in garter st for 1½"/4cm, dec 4 (4, 6, 6, 8, 8) sts evenly spaced across last row—95 (107, 119, 131, 143, 155) sts.

Beg lace pat

Row 1 (RS) Work 2 sts in garter st, work 3 sts in St st, work 12-st rep of lace pat 7 (8, 9, 10, 11, 12) times, k1 (last st of chart), work 3 sts in St st, work 2 sts in garter st. Cont in pats as established until piece measures 13 (13½, 14, 14, 14½, 14½)"/33 (34.5, 35.5, 35.5, 37, 37)cm from beg.

Armhole detail

Next row (RS) Work 5 sts in garter st, cont in pats as established to last 5 sts, work last 5 sts in garter st. Cont in pats as established until piece measures 21½ (22½, 23½, 24, 25, 25½)"/54.5 (57.5, 59.5, 61, 63.5, 65)cm from beg.

Shape shoulder

Bind off 9 (12, 13, 15, 17, 19) sts at beg of next 2 rows, 10 (11, 14, 15, 18, 19) sts at beg of next 4 rows. Bind off rem 37 (39, 37, 41, 37, 41) sts for back neck.

FRONT

Cast on 99 (111, 125, 137, 151, 163) sts. Work in garter st for 1½"/4cm.

Beg lace pat and St st

Row 1 (RS) Work 2 sts in garter st, work 3 sts in St st, work 12-st rep of lace pat 2 (2, 3, 3, 4, 4) times, work in St st over next 40 (52, 42, 54, 44, 56) sts, work 12-st rep of lace pat 2 (2, 3, 3, 4, 4) times, k1 (last st of chart), work 3 sts in St st, work 2 sts in garter st. Cont in pats as established until piece measures 13 (13½, 14, 14, 14½, 14½)"/33 (34.5, 35.5, 35.5, 37, 37)cm from beg. Work armhole detail same as back. Work even until piece measures 15 (15½, 16½, 16½, 17½, 18)"/38 (39.5, 42, 42, 44.5, 45.5) cm from beg.

Shape V-neck

Next row (RS) Work 49 (55, 62, 68, 75, 81) sts, slip next (center) st to a holder or safety pin, join a 2nd ball of yarn and work rem 49 (55, 62, 68, 75, 81) sts. Working both sides at once, work as foll: Work 1 row even.
Next row (RS) Work to last 2 sts on first half, k2tog; on 2nd half, SKP, work to end. Rep last 2 rows 19 (21, 20, 22, 21, 23) times more, AT THE SAME TIME, when piece measures 21½ (22½, 23½, 24, 25, 25½)"/54.5 (57.5, 59.5, 61, 63.5, 65)cm from beg, bind off from each

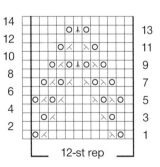

STITCH KEY

☐ k on RS, p on WS

☒ k2tog   ☐ yo

☒ SKP   ☐ S2KP

Rose Callahan

shoulder edge 9 (11, 13, 15, 17, 19) sts once, 10 (11, 14, 15, 18, 19) sts twice.

FINISHING
Sew shoulder seams.

Neckband
With RS facing and circular needle, beg at left shoulder, pick up and k 35 (37, 37, 40, 40, 40) sts along left neck, k1 from holder, pick up 35 (37, 37, 40, 40, 40) sts along right neck and 37 (39, 37, 41, 37, 41) sts along back neck—108 (114, 112, 122, 118, 122) sts. Join and place marker for beg of rnd and work in garter st (p 1 rnd, k 1 rnd) as foll:
Dec rnd K to 1 st before center front st, SK2P, k to end. Rep dec rnd every other rnd, until band measures ¾"/2cm. Bind off. Sew side seams to armhole ribbing.

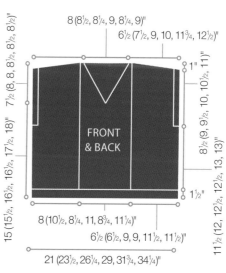

8 (8½, 8¼, 9, 8¼, 9)"

6½ (7½, 9, 10, 11¾, 12½)"

7½ (8, 8, 8½, 8½, 8½)"

15 (15½, 16½, 16½, 17½, 18)"

1"

8½ (9, 9½, 10, 10½, 11)"

FRONT & BACK

1½"

11½ (12, 12½, 12½, 13, 13)"

8 (10½, 8¼, 11, 8¾, 11¼)"

6½ (6½, 9, 9, 11½, 11½)"

21 (23½, 26¼, 29, 31¾, 34¼)"

LACE vest

You'll Need

YARN 3

- 10½oz/300g (14oz/400g, 17½oz/500g) or 700yd/640m (930yd/850m, 1160yd/1060m) of any DK weight acrylic blend

NEEDLES

- One pair each size 6 (4mm) needles *or size to obtain gauge*
- One size 6 (4mm) circular needle, 36"/92cm long

OTHER MATERIALS

- Stitch markers

SIZES

Sized for Small/Medium, Large/X-Large, 1X/2X. Shown in size Small/Medium.

KNITTED MEASUREMENTS

Bust (closed) 34 (44, 53)"/86 (111.5, 134.5)cm
Length 25 (26½, 27½)"/63.5 (67, 70) cm

GAUGE

18 sts and 28 rows to 4"/10cm over lace pat after blocking using size 6 (4mm) needles.
Take time to check gauge.

STITCH GLOSSARY

S2KP Sl 2 sts as for k2tog, k the next st, pass the 2 sl sts over the k st one at a time.
SPP Sl 1 st purlwise, p1, pass slipped st over p1.

Short row wrap & turn (w&t)
on RS row (on WS row)
1 Wyib (wyif), sl next st purlwise.
2 Move yarn between the needles to the front (back).
3 Sl the same st back to LH needle. Turn work. One st is wrapped.
4 When working the wrapped st, insert RH needle under the wrap and work it tog with the corresponding st on needle.

LACE PATTERN

(multiple of 10 sts plus 1)
Note Work lace pat from written instructions below OR foll chart pat.
Row 1 (RS) K2tog, *k3, yo, k1, yo, k3, S2KP; rep from *, end last rep k2tog instead of S2KP.
Rows 2 and 4 Purl.
Row 3 K2tog, *k2, yo, k3, yo, k2, S2KP; rep from *, end last rep k2tog instead of S2KP.
Row 5 K2tog, *[k1, yo] twice, S2KP, [yo, k1] twice, S2KP; rep from *, end last rep k2tog instead of S2KP.
Row 6 Purl.
Rep rows 1-6 for lace pat

LOWER BACK

Cast on 81 (101, 121) sts. P 2 rows. Then beg with RS row 1 work in lace pat for 16 (15, 14)"/40.5 (38.5, 35.5)cm measured from the lowest point. Bind off.

UPPER RIGHT BACK

Cast on 41 (51, 61) sts for center back edge (see schematic). P 2 rows. Then beg with RS row 1, work in lace pat for 6½ (8, 9¼)"/16.5 (20.5, 23.5)cm, end with a RS row.

Shape armhole

Next row (WS) Bind off 25 (33, 41) sts, work to end.
Dec row (RS) K2tog, work to end of row.
Rep dec row every other row 4 (6, 8) times more—11 sts. Work even until piece measures 8½ (11, 13¼)"/21.5 (28, 33.5)cm from beg (measured at the longest unshaped edge). Bind off 11 sts.

UPPER LEFT BACK

Cast on 41 (51, 61) sts for center back edge (see schematic). P 2 rows. Then, beg with RS row 1, work in lace pat for 6½ (8, 9¼)"/16.5 (20.5, 23.5)cm, end with a WS row.

Shape armhole

Next row (RS) Bind off 25 (33, 34) sts, work to end.
Dec row (RS) Work lace pat to the last 2 sts, SKP.
Rep dec row every other row 4 (6, 8) times more—11 sts. Complete as for upper right back.

LEFT FRONT

Cast on 41 (51, 61) sts. Purl 2 rows. Then beg with RS row 1, work in lace pat for 16"/40.5cm.

Shape neck

Note Place a marker to mark the first 12 (14, 16) neck edge sts on the last WS row so that simultaneous neck and armhole shaping is easier to follow.
Next dec row (RS) Work lace pat to the last 2 sts, k2tog.
Rep dec row every other row 11 (13, 15) times more, AT THE SAME TIME, when piece measures 18½ (17½, 16½)"/47 (44.5, 42)cm from beg, end with a WS row, work as foll:

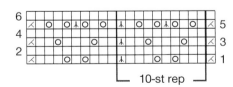

STITCH KEY

☐ k on RS, p on WS
⊠ k2tog
⊙ yo
⊥ S2KP

Rose Callahan

LACE vest

Shape armhole

Bind off from armhole edge as foll: 4 (5, 7) sts once, 4 (3, 3) sts once, 3 sts 1 (2, 3) times.
When all shaping is complete, work even on rem 18 (23, 26) sts until armhole edge measures 6½ (9, 11)"/16.5 (23, 28)cm. Bind off.

RIGHT FRONT

Work as for left front reversing all shaping by working neck decs as SPP at end of WS rows and working armhole shaping at beg of WS rows.

FINISHING

Block pieces to measurements. Join the upper left and right back pieces along the cast-on edges. Sew lower back piece along the bound-off edge to the joined upper back, first centering piece, then easing slightly to fit. Sew shoulder seams leaving an opening of 5 (6, 7)"/12.5 (15, 18)cm for the back neck edge

Armhole trim

Pick up and k 66 (90, 110) sts evenly around armhole opening.
Next row *K1, p1; rep from * to end.
Short row 1 Work in k1, p1 rib to the last 8 sts, w&t.
Short row 2 Rep short row 1.
Short row 3 Work in rib to the last 16 sts, w&t.
Short row 4 Rep short row 3.
Next 2 rows Work to end of row, closing up the wraps. Bind off knitwise. Sew side and trim seams.

Front and neck band trim

With circular needle, beg at lower right front, pick up and k 82 sts to the neck edge, pm, 38 (44, 48) sts to the back neck, pm, 22 (26, 32) sts across the back neck, pm, 38 (44, 48) sts to the end of the left neck edge, pm, 82 sts to the lower left front—262 (278, 292) total sts.
Row 1 (WS) Work in k1, p1 rib.
Row 2 (RS) Work in rib to the first neck marker, inc 1 st in rib, sl marker, inc 1 st in rib, work in rib to the back neck marker, SKP, sl marker, k2tog, work in rib to the 2nd back neck marker, SKP, sl marker, k2tog, work in rib to the left neck marker, inc 1 st in rib, sl marker, inc 1 st in rib, work in rib to end.
Rep the last 2 rows twice more. Work 1 row in rib. Bind off knitwise. Block finished piece lightly.

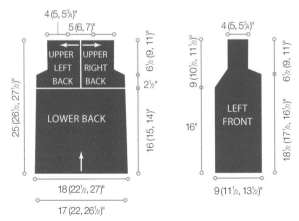

PLACKET pullover

You'll Need

YARN ③

- 17½oz/500g (21oz/600g, 24½oz/700g, 28oz/800g, 28oz/800g, 31½oz/900g) or 1030yd/940 (1230yd/ 1130m, 1440yd/1310m, 1640yd/1500m, 1640yd/ 1500m, 1850yd/1690m) of any DK weight cotton in yellow (MC)
- 7oz/200g (7oz/200g, 10½oz/300g, 10½oz/300g, 14oz/400g, 14oz/400g) or 410yd/380m (410yd/380m, 620yd/570m, 620yd/570m, 820yd/750m, 820yd/ 750m) in white (CC)

NEEDLES

- One size 6 (4mm) circular needle, 32"/80cm length *or size to obtain gauge*
- One size 6 (4mm) circular needle, 16"/40cm length

OTHER MATERIALS

- 4 stitch markers, scrap yarn or stitch holders

ul Amato. lvarepresents.com

SIZES

Sized for Small, Medium, Large, 1X, 2X and 3X. Shown in size Small.

KNITTED MEASUREMENTS

Bust 36 (40, 43¼, 48, 52, 56)"/91.5 (101.5, 110, 122, 132, 142)cm
Length 24 (24¾, 26, 26¾, 28, 28½)"/61 (63, 66, 68, 71, 72.5) cm
Upper arm 12½ (14, 15, 16, 17, 18)"/32 (35.5, 38, 40.5, 43, 45.5)cm

GAUGES

22 sts and 28 rows to 4"/10cm over St st using size 6 (4mm) needle.
21 sts and 28 rows to 4"/10cm over seed st using size 6 (4mm) needle.
Take time to check gauges.

NOTES

1 When changing colors, twist yarns on WS to prevent holes in work.
2 Use a separate bobbin for each color section. Do not carry yarn across back of work.
3 Sweater is worked in one piece from the neck down.

STITCH GLOSSARY

Seed stitch
Row 1 *K1, p1; rep from * to end.
Row 2 K the purl sts and p the knit sts.
Rep row 2 for seed st.

PULLOVER

With longer circular needle and CC, cast on 78 (82, 90, 94, 96, 106) sts for collar edge. Work in seed st for 13 rows.
Next row (WS) Working in seed st, work first 8 sts, inc 10 sts evenly to last 8 sts, work last 8 sts—88 (92, 100, 104, 106, 116) sts.

YOKE

Row 1 (RS) With CC, work in seed st for

PLACKET *pullover*

8 sts, attach MC and working in St st, k10 (12, 13, 16, 17, 20) sts, place marker (pm), k7 (6, 7, 4, 2, 2) sleeve sts, pm, k38 (40, 44, 48, 52, 56) back sts, pm, k7 (6, 7, 4, 2, 2) sleeve sts, pm, k10 (12, 13, 16, 17, 20) sts, attach second ball of CC and k last 8 sts in seed st.

Row 2 (WS) With CC, work 8 sts in seed st, with MC and slipping markers, purl to last 8 sts, with CC, work last 8 sts in seed st.

Row 3 (inc row) With CC, work 8 sts in seed st, with MC, *k to 1 st before marker, k into front and back of next st (kfb), slip marker (sl m), kfb; rep from * 3 times more, knit to last 8 sts, with CC, work last 8 sts in seed st.

Rep inc row every other row 28 (29, 32, 35, 34, 36) times more, then every row 0 (3, 3, 4, 9, 10) times, working WS inc rows as foll:

Inc row 2 (WS) With CC, work 8 sts in seed st, with MC, *p to 1 st before marker, p into front and back of next st (pfb), slip marker (sl m), pfb; rep from * 3 times more, purl to last 8 sts, with CC, work last 8 sts in seed st.

After all incs are worked yoke should have 320 (356, 388, 424, 458, 492) sts.

Separate yoke

With CC, work 8 sts in seed st, with MC, k39 (45, 49, 56, 61, 67) sts, cast on 2 sts for first half of front, pm, cast on 2 sts, place 65 (72, 79, 84, 90, 96) sleeve sts on holder, k96 (106, 116, 128, 140, 150) sts, cast on 2 sts for back, pm, cast on 2 sts, place 65 (72, 79, 84, 90, 96) sleeve sts on holder, k39 (45, 49, 56, 61, 67) sts, cut CC, with MC, k8 for 2nd half of front, join for knitting in the round, k8, k to marker. Use this marker as beg of rnd—198 (220, 238, 264, 286, 308) sts.

BODY

With MC work in St st for 3½ (3½, 4, 4, 4½, 4½)"/9 (9, 10, 10, 11.5, 11.5)cm from armhole edge.

Split for front and back

Next row With CC, work 8 sts in seed st, attach MC, work in St st to 8 sts before 2nd marker, attach 2nd ball of CC, work 8 sts in seed st, place rem 98 (110, 118, 132, 142, 154) front sts on holder.

Work back and forth in rows over center 100 (110, 120, 132, 144, 154) sts for back in pats as established for 10 (10, 10½, 10½, 11, 11)"/25.5, 25.5, 26.5, 26.5, 28, 28)cm from beg of armhole, end with a WS row.

With CC, k next row on RS, then work in pats as established for 4"/10cm. Bind off in pat.

FRONT

Replace sts to needle. Work as for Back.

SLEEVES

With MC and shorter circular needle, cast on 2 sts, k sts from one sleeves holder, cast on 2 sts—69 (76, 83, 88, 94, 100) sts. Place marker and join for knitting in the round. Work in St st until piece measures 3"/7.5cm from armhole edge.

Next row With CC, work 8 sts in seed st, attach MC, work in St st to 8 sts before marker, attach 2nd ball of CC, work 8 st in seed st.

Work in rows in pats as established until piece measures 6"/15cm from armhole edge.

Next row With CC, work across all sts in seed st. Work in pats as established until piece measures 9"/23cm from armhole edge.

FINISHING

Graft underarm sts together.
With CC, sew up 1"/2.5cm of seed st trim at sides and sleeves.
With CC, sew up 2"/5cm of seed st trim at neck placket.

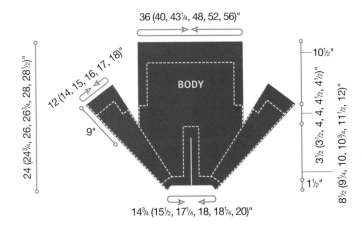

NAUTICAL plunge

You'll Need

YARN 3

- *Microspun* by Lion Brand Co., 2½oz/70g balls, each approx 164yd/154m (microfiber/acrylic)
- 2 (3, 3) balls in #109 royal blue (A)
- 2 (3, 3) balls in #100 lily white (B)

NEEDLES

- One pair each sizes 3 and 4 (3 and 3.5mm) knitting needles *or sizes to obtain gauge*

OTHER

- Size D/3 (3.25mm) crochet hook

SIZES

Sized for Small, Medium, Large. Shown in size Small.

KNITTED MEASUREMENTS

Bust 32 (36, 40)"/81 (91.5, 101.5)cm
Length 20½ (22, 23½)"/52 (56, 59.5) cm

GAUGE

24 sts and 32 rows to 4"/10cm over St st using smaller needles.
Take time to check gauge.

STITCH GLOSSARY

Ribbed Border
Row 1 (RS) P4, k to last 4 sts, p4.
Row 2 K4, p to last 4 sts, k4.
Row 3 Knit.

Row 4 Purl.
Rep rows 1–4 for ribbed border.

Stripe Pattern
Working in St st, *work 14 rows B, 14 rows A; rep from * (24 rows) for stripe pat.

BACK

With smaller needles and A, cast on 98 (106, 118) sts. Work in k2, p2 rib for 4 rows, inc 0 (2, 2) sts evenly spaced across last row—98 (108, 120) sts. Change to larger needles and St st and work even for 10 rows. Cont in stripe pat and work even until piece measures 12 (13, 14)"/30.5 (33, 35.5)cm from beg, end with a WS row.

Shape armholes
Dec row (RS) K2, k2tog, k to last 4 sts, ssk, k2. Purl next row. Rep last 2 rows 7 times more—82 (92, 104) sts.

Armhole bands
Cont in ribbed border, AT THE SAME TIME, inc 1 st after first 4 rib sts and 1 st before last 4 rib sts on first row, then every other row 5 (5, 3) times more, every 4th row 7 (8, 10) times—108 (120, 132) sts. Work even until armhole measures 7½ (8, 8½)"/10 (20.5, 21.5) cm, end with a WS row.

Shape shoulders
Bind off 8 (9, 10) sts at beg of next 4 rows, then 7 (9, 11) sts at beg of next 4 rows. Bind off rem 48 sts for back neck.

FRONT

Lower front
Work as for back until piece measures 10 (11, 12)"/25.5 (28, 30.5)cm from beg, end with a WS row.

Shape bodice
Bind off 12 (14, 14) sts at beg of next 2 rows, then 11 (12, 14) sts at beg of next 6

rows. Bind off rem 8 sts.

Upper left front
With smaller needles and A, cast on 58 (62, 66) sts. Work in k2, p2 rib for 4 rows, inc 2 (2, 0) sts evenly spaced across last row—60 (64, 66) sts.

Shape shoulder and bodice edges
Note Read through entire shaping instructions before you begin to knit. Change to larger needles and St st. Work for 10 rows, AT THE SAME TIME, inc 1 st at beg (bodice edge) on first row and dec 1 st at end (shoulder edge) on first (5th, 5th) and 7th (0, 0) rows. Cont in stripe pat and inc 1 st at beg (bodice edge) on first row, then every 8th (10th, 12th) row 4 times more. AT THE SAME TIME, when 2 (0, 2) rows of stripe pat have been completed, cont to shape

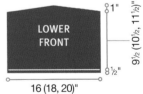

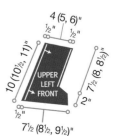

shoulder by dec 1 st at end of next row, then every 6th (6th, 8th) row 3 (4, 4) times more. Work until piece measures 4½ (5½, 6½)"/11.5 (14, 16.5)cm from beg, end with a WS row.

Armhole band
Row 1 (RS) K to last 40 (44, 48) sts, [p2, k2] 10 (11, 12) times.
Row 2 [P2, k2] 10 (11, 12) times, p to end. Rep row 1 once more.
Next row (WS) Bind off first 42 (46, 48) sts, p to end—18 sts.

Shape armhole
Dec row (RS) K to last 4 sts, ssk, k2. Purl next row. Rep last 2 rows 5 times more; piece should measure 8 (9, 10)"/20.5 (23, 25.5)cm from beg. Bind off rem 12 sts.

Upper right front
Work as for upper left front, reversing all shaping to shape armhole—18 sts.

Shape armhole
Dec row (RS) K2, k2tog, k to end. Purl next row. Rep last 2 rows 5 times more. Bind off rem 12 sts.

FINISHING
Sew bottom edges of upper left and right fronts to bodice of lower front. Sew shoulder and side seams.

Back neck edging
With RS facing and crochet hook, join A with a sl st in right shoulder seam. **Row 1** Ch 1, sc in each st across to left shoulder seam. Fasten off.

Nick Norwood

MESH hoodie

You'll Need

YARN (4)

- 14⅘oz/420g (15⅗oz/455g, 18oz/525g, 20⅘oz/595g, 22⅘oz/665g, 26⅔oz/770g, 28⅘oz/840g) or 1200yd/1080 (1300yd/1170m, 1500yd/1350m, 1700yd/1530m, 1900yd/1710m, 2200yd/1980m, 2400yd/2160m) of any worsted weight cotton

NEEDLES

- One pair each size 7 and 8 (4.5 and 5mm) needles *or size to obtain gauge.*
- Spare size 8 (5mm) needle for 3-needle bind-off
- Size 7 and 8 (4.5 and 5mm) circular needles, 24"/61cm long
- Two size 7 (4.5mm) double-pointed needles (dpns) for I-cord

OTHER

- Size G/6 (4mm) crochet hook
- Stitch holders

SIZES

Sized for X-Small, Small, Medium, Large, 1X, 2X, 3X. Shown in size Small.

KNITTED MEASUREMENTS

Bust (closed) 34 (38, 42½, 47, 51, 55½, 59½)"/86.5 (96.5, 108, 119.5, 129.5, 141, 151)cm
Length 24½ (25, 25½, 27, 27½, 29, 29½"/62 (63.5, 64.5, 68.5, 70, 73.5, 75)cm
Upper arm 13 (14, 15, 16, 17, 18, 19)"/33 (35.5, 38, 40.5, 43, 45.5, 48)cm

GAUGE

15 sts and 24 rows to 4"/10cm over pat st using larger needles.
Take time to check gauge.

STITCH GLOSSARY

3-needle bind-off

1 With WS tog, hold pieces on two parallel needles so both tips point right. Insert 3rd needle knitwise into first st of each needle and wrap yarn around each needle as if to knit.
2 Knit these 2 sts tog and sl them off the needles. *K the next 2 sts tog in the same manner.
3 Sl first st on 3rd needle over the 2nd st and off the needle. Rep from * in step 2 across row until all sts are bound off.

Pattern stitch (multiple of 4 sts)
Row 1 (RS) K4, *yo twice, k4; rep from * to end.
Row 2 P2, *p2tog, work (p1, k1) in double yo, p2tog; rep from * to end.
Row 3 K2, yo, *k4, yo twice; rep from *, end k4, yo, k2.
Row 4 P3, *[p2tog] twice, work (p1, k1) in double yo; rep from *, end [p2tog] twice, p3.
Rep rows 1–4 for pat st.

BACK

With smaller needles, cast on 64 (72, 80, 88, 96, 104, 112) sts. Work in garter st for 4 rows. Change to larger circular needle. Work back and forth in pat st until piece measures 18 (18, 18, 19, 19, 20, 20)"/45.5 (45.5, 45.5, 48, 48, 51, 51)cm from beg, end with row 2.

Shape sleeves
Next row (RS) Cast on 20 (20, 20, 20, 24, 24, 24) sts, k cast-on sts, work row 3 to end.
Next row Cast on 20 (20, 20, 20, 24, 24, 24) sts, p cast-on sts, work row 4 to last 20 (20, 20, 20, 24, 24, 24) sts, p to end—104 (112, 120, 128, 144, 152, 160) sts. Beg with row 1, cont in pat st on all sts until sleeve measures 6½ (7, 7½, 8, 8½, 9, 9½)"/16.5 (17.5, 19, 20.5, 21.5, 23, 24)cm, end with a WS row. Place first 32 (36, 40, 44, 52, 56, 60) sts on holder for right back sleeve, place center 40 sts on holder for back neck, place last 32 (36, 40, 44, 52, 56, 60) sts on holder for left back sleeve.

LEFT FRONT

With smaller needles, cast on 32 (36, 40, 44, 48, 52, 56) sts. Work in garter st for 4 rows. Change to larger circular needle. Work back and forth in pat st until piece measures 18 (18, 18, 19, 19, 20, 20)"/45.5 (45.5, 45.5, 48, 48, 51, 51)cm from beg, end with row 2.

Shape sleeve
Next row (RS) Cast on 20 (20, 20, 20, 24, 24, 24) sts, k cast-on sts, work row 3 to end. **Next row** Work row 4 to last 20 (20, 20, 20, 24, 24, 24) sts, p to end—52 (56, 60, 64, 72, 76, 80) sts. Beg with row 1, cont in pat st on all sts until sleeve measures same length as back to shoulder, end with a WS row. Place first 32 (36, 40, 44, 52, 56, 60) sts on holder for left front sleeve, place last 20 sts on holder for front neck.

RIGHT FRONT

Work same as left front to shape sleeve, end with row 3.

Shape sleeve
Next row (WS) Cast on 20 (20, 20, 20, 24, 24, 24) sts, p cast-on sts, work row 4 to end—52 (56, 60, 64, 72, 76, 80) sts. Beg with row 1, cont in pat st on all sts until sleeve measures same length as back to shoulder, end with a WS row. Place first 20 sts on holder for front neck, place last 32 (36, 40, 44, 52, 56, 60) sts on holder for right front sleeve.

FINISHING

Block pieces to measurements. For left sleeve and shoulder, place 32 (36, 40, 44, 52, 56, 60) sts from left back sleeve holder on a larger needle ready for a

Rose Callahan

front edge—374 (380, 386, 400, 406, 420, 426) sts. **Rows 1–6** Knit. **Row 7** Purl. **Row 8** Knit. Bind off all sts loosely purlwise. Fold frontband in half to WS and sew in place.

I-cord tie
With dpn, cast on 4 sts leaving a long tail. Work in I-cord as foll:
***Next row (RS)** With 2nd dpn, k4, do not turn. Slide sts back to beg of needle to work next row from RS; rep from * until I-cord measures 63 (66, 69, 73, 77, 81, 85)"/160 (167.5, 175, 185.5, 195.5, 205.5, 216)cm from beg. Cut yarn leaving a long tail. Thread tail into tapestry needle, then weave needle through sts. Pull tail to gather; fasten off securely. Rep for opposite end. Weave tie through sts around waist.

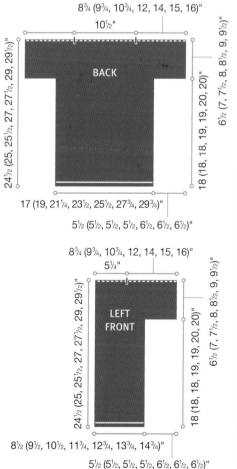

WS row. Place 32 (36, 40, 44, 52, 56, 60) sts from left front sleeve holder on a larger needle ready for a RS row. With WS tog, hold pieces on two parallel needles. Cont to work 3-needle bind-off. For right sleeve and shoulder, place 32 (36, 40, 44, 52, 56, 60) sts from right back sleeve holder on a larger needle ready for a RS row. Place 32 (36, 40, 44, 52, 56, 60) sts from right front sleeve holder on a larger needle ready for a WS row. With WS tog, hold pieces on two parallel needles. Cont to work 3-needle bind-off.

Hood
With RS facing, place 20 sts from right front neck holder, 40 sts from back neck holder and 20 sts from left neck holder on smaller circular needle. Cont to work back and forth in pat st for 8 rows. Change to larger circular needle. Cont

in pat st for 12"/30.5cm, end with a WS row. Bind off knitwise. Fold hood in half and sew seam.

Sleeve edging
With RS facing and smaller needles, pick up and k 49 (53, 56, 60, 64, 68, 71) sts evenly spaced along sleeve edge. Work in garter st for 2 rows. Bind off all sts knitwise. Sew side and sleeve seams.

Bottom edging
With RS facing and crochet hook, join yarn with a sl st in bottom edge of first st. **Row 1 (RS)** Ch 1, then sc in bottom edge of each st across. Fasten off.

Front band
With RS facing and smaller circular needle, pick up and k 122 (125, 128, 135, 138, 145, 148) sts along right front edge, 130 sts along hood edge, then 122 (125, 128, 135, 138, 145, 148) sts along left

LEMON made

You'll Need

SIZES

Sized for Small, Medium, Large, 1X, 2X, 3X. Shown in size Small.

KNITTED MEASUREMENTS

Bust 34 (38, 42, 46, 50, 54)"/86.5 (96.5, 106.5, 117, 127, 137)cm
Length 20 (20½, 21½, 22½, 23½, 24)"/51 (52, 54.5, 57, 59.5, 61)cm
Upper arm 9½ (10½, 11½, 12½, 13½, 14½)"/24 (26.5, 29, 31.5, 34, 37)cm

GAUGE

24 sts and 32 rows to 4"/10cm over St st using larger needles.
Take time to check gauge.

BACK

With larger needles, cast on 102 (114, 126, 138, 150, 162) sts. Work in St st for 4 rows, end with a WS row.
Next (picot) row (RS) K1, *yo, k2tog; rep from *, end k1. Beg with a p row,

cont in St st until piece measures 3½ (3½, 4, 4½, 5, 5)"/9 (9, 10, 11.5, 12.5, 12.5)cm above picot row, end with a WS row.

Shape waist

Next row (RS) K25 (29, 33, 36, 39, 42), pm, k52 (56, 60, 66, 72, 78), pm, k25 (29, 33, 36, 39, 42). Purl next row.
Next (dec) row (RS) *K to 3 sts before marker, ssk, k1, sl marker, k1, k2tog; rep from * once more, k to end. Rep dec row every 8th row twice more—90 (102, 114, 126, 138, 150) sts. Work even until piece measures 6½ (6½, 7, 7½, 8, 8)"/16.5 (16.5, 17.5, 19, 20.5, 20.5)cm above picot row, end with a WS row.
Next (inc) row (RS) *K to 1 st before marker, M1, k1, sl marker, k1, M1; rep from * once more, k to end. Rep inc row every 10th row twice more—102 (114, 126, 138, 150, 162) sts. Work even until piece measures 12 (12, 12½, 13, 13½, 13½)"/30.5 (30.5, 31.5, 33, 34, 34)cm above picot row, end with a WS row.

Shape armholes

Bind off 5 (6, 7, 8, 9, 10) sts at beg of next 2 rows, then 3 (4, 5, 5, 6, 6) sts at beg of next 2 rows. Mark beg and end of last row for cap sleeve placement. Dec 1 st each side on next row, then every other row 2 (3, 4, 6, 7, 9) times more. Work even on 80 (86, 92, 98, 104, 110) sts until armhole measures 7 (7½, 8, 8½, 9, 9½)"/17.5 (19, 20.5, 21.5, 23, 24) cm, end with a WS row.

Shape shoulders and neck

Bind off 7 (8, 8, 9, 11, 12) sts at beg of next 2 rows, then 7 (8, 9, 10, 10, 11) sts at beg of next 4 rows. AT THE SAME TIME, bind off center 24 (24, 26, 26, 28, 28) sts for neck, then bind off 7 sts from each neck edge once.

FRONT

Work as for back until piece measures 11½ (11½, 12, 12½, 13, 13)"/29 (29, 30.5, 31.5, 33, 33)cm above picot row,

end with a WS row—102 (114, 126, 138, 150, 162) sts.

Divide for placket opening

Next row (RS) K25 (29, 33, 37, 41, 45), pm, k25 (27, 29, 31, 33, 35), join a 2nd ball of yarn, bind off center 2 sts, k until there are 25 (27, 29, 31, 33, 35) sts on RH needle, pm, k25 (29, 33, 37, 41, 45). Work both sides at once as foll:

Beg broken rib pat

Next row (WS) P to marker, sl marker, p22 (24, 26, 28, 30, 32), k1, p2; with 2nd ball, p2, k1, p to end. Knit next row. Rep last 2 rows once more. Cont broken rib pat as foll:

Shape armholes

Next row (RS) Bind off 5 (6, 7, 8, 9, 10) sts, k to end; with 2nd ball of yarn, k to end.
Next row Bind off 5 (6, 7, 8, 9, 10) sts, p to marker, sl marker, p20 (22, 24, 26, 28, 30), k1, p1, k1, p2; with 2nd ball, p2, k1, p1, k1, p to end.
Next row (RS) Bind off 3 (4, 5, 5, 6, 6) sts, k to end; with 2nd ball of yarn, k to end.
Next row Bind off 3 (4, 5, 5, 6, 6) sts, p to marker, sl marker, p20 (22, 24, 26, 28, 30), k1, p1, k1, p2; with 2nd ball, p2, k1, p1, k1, p to end. Mark beg and end of

Paul Amato lvarepresents.com

last row for sleeve placement.

Next row (RS) Ssk, k to end; with 2nd ball of yarn, k to last 2 sts, k2tog.

Next row P to marker, sl marker, p18 (20, 22, 24, 26, 28), [k1, p1] twice, k1, p2; with 2nd ball of yarn, p2, [k1, p1] twice, k1, p to end. Rep last 2 rows once more. Cont to dec 1 st each side every other row 1 (2, 3, 5, 6, 8) times more. AT THE SAME TIME, cont to work 2 more broken rib sts each side every 4th row 9 (10, 11, 12, 13, 14) times more; then cont to work broken rib and St st as established to the end. When armhole shaping is completed, work even on 39 (42, 45, 48, 51, 54) sts each side until armhole measures 5 (5½, 6, 6½, 7, 7½)"/12.5 (14, 15, 16.5, 17.5, 19)cm, end with a WS row.

Shape neck

Bind off 7 (7, 8, 8, 9, 9) sts each neck edge once, 5 sts once, 3 sts once, 2 sts once, then 1 st once. Work even on 21 (24, 26, 29, 31, 34) sts each side until piece measures same length as back to shoulders, end with a WS row. Shape shoulders as for back.

CAP SLEEVES

With larger needles, cast on 52 (58, 64, 70, 76, 82) sts. Knit next row. Beg with a p row, cont in St st and inc 1 st each side every row 3 times—58 (64, 70, 76, 82, 88) sts.

Next (picot) row (RS) K1, *yo, k2tog; rep from *, end k1. Beg with a p row, cont in St st and dec 1 st each side every row 3 times—52 (58, 64, 70, 76, 82) sts.

Shape cap

Bind off 1 st at beg of next 18 (18, 16, 16, 14, 14) rows, then 2 sts at beg of next 14 (16, 20, 22, 26, 28) rows. Bind off rem 6 (8, 8, 10, 10, 12) sts.

FINISHING

Block pieces to measurements. Sew shoulder seams.

Button placket

With RS facing and smaller needles, pick up and k 36 sts evenly spaced along left front placket opening. Work in garter st for 5 rows. Bind off all sts knitwise.

Buttonhole placket

With RS facing and smaller needles, pick up and k 36 sts evenly spaced along right front placket opening. Work in garter st for 2 rows.

Next (buttonhole) row (WS) K2, yo, k2tog, *k4, yo, k2tog; rep from * 4 times more, end k2. Cont in garter st for 2 rows. Bind off all sts knitwise. Lap buttonhole placket over button placket and sew bottom edge in place. On WS, tack bottom edge of button placket in place.

Neckband

With RS facing and smaller needles, pick up and k 90 (90, 94, 94, 98, 98) sts evenly spaced along entire neck edge. Beg with a p row, cont in St st for 3 rows.

Next (picot) row (RS) K1, *yo, k2tog; rep from *, end k1. Beg with a p row, cont in St st for 3 rows. Bind off. Fold neckband in half to WS along picot row and hem in place. Fold bottom edge of each cap sleeve to WS along picot row and hem in place. Sew on cap sleeves between armhole markers. Sew side seams. Fold bottom edge of front and back to WS along picot row and hem in place. Sew on buttons.

MESH cardigan

You'll Need

YARN 4

- 14oz/400g (17½oz/500g, 17½oz/500g, 21oz/600g, 21oz/600g, 21oz/600g, 24½oz/700g) of any worsted weight bamboo blend yarn

NEEDLES

- One pair each size 5 (3.75mm) needles *or size to obtain gauge*
- One size 5 (3.75mm) circular needle, 32"/81cm long

OTHER MATERIALS

- Four ³/₈"/1cm buttons
- Stitch markers, stitch holders

SIZES

Sized for Small, Medium, Large, X-Large, 1X, 2X, 3X. Shown in size Small.

KNITTED MEASUREMENTS

Bust (closed) 35½ (37, 41½, 44¼, 47¼, 49½, 53)"/90 (94, 105.5, 112.5, 120, 125.5, 134.5)cm
Length 21½ (22, 22¼, 22½, 22½, 23, 23½)"/54 (56, 56.5, 57, 57, 58.5, 59.5)cm
Upper arm 14½ (16¼, 17, 18½, 20¼, 21¾, 23½)"/37 (41, 43, 47, 51.5, 55, 59.5)cm
Note Selvage sts are not included in the measurements.

GAUGE

20 sts and 32 rows to 4"/10cm over mesh stripe pat using size 5 (3.75mm) needles.
Take time to check gauge.

3-NEEDLE BIND-OFF

1 Hold right sides of pieces together on two needles. Insert third needle knitwise into first st of each needle, and wrap yarn knitwise.
2 Knit these two sts together, and slip them off the needles. *Knit the next two sts together in the same manner.
3 Slip first st on 3rd needle over 2nd st and off needle. Rep from * in step 2 across row until all sts are bound off.

MESH STRIPE PAT

(multiple of 4 sts plus 3, plus 2 selvage sts)
Note Work mesh stripe pat from written instructions below OR foll chart pat.
Row 1 (RS) K1 (selvage st), k1, yo, SK2P, *yo, k1, yo, SK2P; rep from *, end yo, SKP, yo, k1, k1 (selvage st).
Row 2 and all WS rows Purl.
Row 3 K1 (selvage st), k1, yo, k2tog, *yo, SK2P, yo, k1; rep from *, end k1 (selvage st)
Rows 5 and 9 Rep row 1.
Rows 7 and 11 Rep row 3.
Row 12 Purl.
Row 13 Knit.
Row 14 Purl.
Rep rows 1-14 for mesh stripe pat.

BACK

Cast on 89 (93, 101, 109, 117, 125, 133) sts. Work in garter st (k every row) for 4 rows.

Beg mesh stripe pat

Beg with row 1, work in mesh stripe pat, rep rows 1-14 until piece measures 13 (13, 13, 13, 12½, 12½, 12½)"/33 (33, 33, 33, 32, 32, 32)cm from beg. Place markers at each side of last row to mark for armholes.
Work even until piece measures 8 (8½, 8¾, 9, 9½, 10, 10½)"/20.5 (21.5, 22, 23, 24, 25.5, 26.5)cm from the markers.

Shape neck

Next row (RS) Work 26 (28, 32, 36, 39, 43, 47) sts, join a 2nd ball of yarn and bind off center 37 (37, 37, 37, 39, 39, 39) sts, work to end. Working both sides at once, dec 1 st at each neck edge on next row. Work even until armhole measures 8½ (9, 9¼, 9½, 10, 10½, 11)"/21.5 (23, 23.5, 24, 25.5, 26.5, 28)cm. Sl the rem 25 (27, 31, 35, 38, 42, 46) sts each side to st holders for shoulders.

LEFT FRONT

Cast on 45 (49, 53, 57, 61, 65, 69) sts. Work in garter st for 4 rows.

Beg mesh stripe pat

Beg with row 1, work in mesh stripe pat, rep rows 1-14 until piece measures 13 (13, 13, 13, 12½, 12½, 12½)"/33 (33, 33, 33, 31.5, 31.5, 31.5)cm from beg. Place marker at beg of next RS row to mark for beg of armhole.
Work even until piece measures 2½ (3, 3¼, 3½, 3½, 4, 4½)"/6.5 (7.5, 8.5, 9, 9, 10, 11.5)cm from the marker.

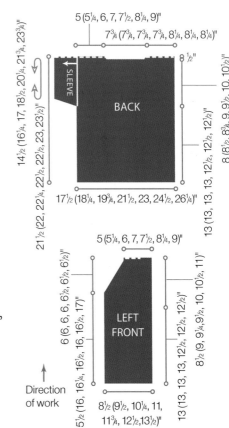

Shape neck

Dec row (RS) Work pat to the last 3 sts, k2tog, k1. Cont in pat and rep dec row every other row 19 (21, 21, 21, 22, 22, 22) times more—25 (27, 31, 35, 38, 42, 46) sts. Work even until armhole measures same as back armhole. Sl the rem sts to a st holder.

RIGHT FRONT

Work as for left front to the neck shaping.

Shape neck

Dec row (RS) K1, SKP, work pat to end. Complete as for left front.

Pre-finishing

Join corresponding shoulders tog from the WS using the 3-needle bind off method.

SLEEVES

Pick up and k 89 (97, 101, 109, 117, 125, 133) sts along one armhole edge, beg and end at the armhole markers. Purl 1 row, then, work rows 1 and 2 in mesh stripe pat.

Dec row (RS) K1, SKP, cont in pat to the last 3 sts, k2tog, k1. Cont in pat and rep dec row every 4th row 6 times more—75 (83, 87, 95, 103, 111, 119) sts. P1 row. K 5 rows. Bind off sts knitwise.

Rose Callahan

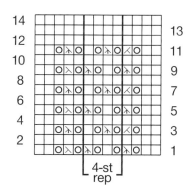

```
14                                    13
12
10    O ⋏ O   O ⋏ O ⋏ O               11
 8      O ⋏ O ⋏ O   O ⋏ O              9
 6      O ⋏ O   O ⋏ O ⋏ O              7
 4      O ⋏ O ⋏ O   O ⋏ O              5
 2      O ⋏ O   O ⋏ O ⋏ O              3
        O ⋏ O ⋏ O   O ⋏ O              1
         └─ 4-st ─┘
            rep
```

STITCH KEY

☐ k on RS, p on WS

⊡ yo   ⊠ k2tog

⊠ SKP   ⋏ SK2P

FINISHING

Block lightly to measurements. Sew side and sleeve seams.

Front and neck bands

From the RS with circular needle, beg at lower right front, pick up and k 98 (100, 102, 104, 100, 102, 104) sts to the beg of the neck shaping, pm, 32 (32, 32, 32, 34, 34, 34) sts to the back neck, 42 (42, 42, 42, 44, 44, 44) sts across the back neck, 32 (32, 32, 32, 34, 34, 34) sts to the left neck shaping, 98 (100, 102, 104, 100, 102, 104) sts to the lower left front—302 (306, 310, 314, 312, 316, 320) sts. K 3 rows.

Buttonhole row (RS) K60 (62, 64, 66, 62, 64, 66), yo, k2tog, [k10, yo, k2tog] 3 times, k to end.

Next row Knit.

Bind off all sts purlwise. Sew on buttons.

FLORAL jacket

You'll Need

YARN 4

- 24oz/700g (24oz/700g, 28oz/800g, 31½oz/900g) or 1150yd/1050m (1150yd/1050m, 1310yd/1200m, 1470yd/1350m) of any worsted weight acrylic blend in white (MC)
- 3½oz/100g or 170yd/150m in each pink (A) and green (B)

NEEDLES

- One pair each sizes 8 and 9 (5 and 5.5mm) needles *or size to obtain gauge*

OTHER MATERIALS

- Size 7 (4.5mm) crochet hook
- 1½"/4cm-long sew-on barpin
- White, pink and green sewing threads (for flower pin)

SIZES

Sized for Small, Medium, Large, X-Large. Shown in size Medium.

KNITTED MEASUREMENTS

Bust (closed) 37 (39, 42½, 45)"/94 (99, 108, 114.5)cm
Length 17½ (18½, 19½, 20½)"/44.5 (47, 49.5, 52)cm
Upper arm 11½ (12½, 13½, 14½)"/29 (31.5, 34, 37)cm

GAUGE

18 sts and 28 rows to 4"/10cm over St st using size 8 (5mm) needles.
Take time to check gauge.

BACK

With larger needles and MC, cast on 84 (88, 96, 102) sts. Change to smaller needles and work in k1, p1 rib for 2 rows. Cont in St st and work even until piece measures 9 (9½, 10, 10½)"/23 (24, 25.5, 26.5)cm from beg, end with a WS row.

Shape armholes

Dec row (RS) K2, k2tog, k to last 4 sts, ssk, k2. Rep dec row every other row 6 (7, 8, 8) times more, then every 4th row 6 times—58 (60, 66, 72) sts. Work even until armhole measures 7 (7½, 8, 8½)"/17.5 (19, 20.5, 21.5)cm, end with a WS row.

Shape neck and shoulders

Next row (RS) K13 (14, 16, 19) sts, join another ball of MC and bind off center 32 (32, 34, 34) sts for back neck, k to end. Working both sides at once, bind off 2 sts from each neck edge once, then dec 1 st every row 3 times, AT THE SAME TIME, when armhole measures 7½ (8, 8½, 9)"/19 (20.5, 21.5, 23)cm, end with a WS row. Bind off from each shoulder edge 2 (3, 3, 4) sts once, then 3 (3, 4, 5) sts twice.

LEFT FRONT

With larger needles and MC, cast on 54 (56, 62, 66) sts. Change to smaller needles and work in k1, p1 rib for 2 rows.

Beg front band

Next row (RS) K48 (50, 56, 60) sts, [p1, k1] 3 times.
Next row [P1, k1] 3 times, p48 (50, 56, 60) sts. Cont to work as established with 6 sts at front edge in rib and rem sts in St st until piece measures 7 (7½, 8, 8½)"/17.5 (19, 20.5, 21.5)cm from beg, end with a WS row. **Next (dec) row** K17 (18, 19, 21) sts, [k2tog] 10 (10, 12, 12) times, k 11 (12, 13, 15) sts, [p1, k1] 3 times—44 (46, 50, 54) sts. Cont to work as established until piece measures same as back to armhole, shape armhole at side edge only as for back, AT THE SAME TIME, when armhole measures 4 (4½, 5, 5½)"/10 (11.5, 12.5, 14)cm, end with a RS row.

Shape neck and shoulder

Next row (WS) Bind off 8 (9, 9, 10) sts, work to end. Cont to bind off 3 sts from neck edge twice, then 2 sts twice.
Dec row (RS) Work to last 3 sts, ssk, k1. Rep dec row every other row 4 times more. Work even until same length as back to shoulder. Shape shoulder at side edge as for back.

RIGHT FRONT

With larger needle and MC, cast on 54 (56, 62, 66) sts. Change to smaller needles and work in k1, p1 rib for 2 rows.

Beg front band

Next row (RS) [P1, k1] 3 times, k48 (50, 56, 60) sts. **Next row** P48 (50, 56, 60) sts, [p1, k1] 3 times. Cont to work as established with 6 sts at front edge in rib and rem sts in St st until piece measures

1¾ (2, 2½, 3)"
9¼ (9¼, 9¾, 9¾)"
1½"
1"
16 (17, 18, 19)"
9 (9½, 10, 10½)"
7½ (8, 8½, 9)"
BACK
18½ (19½, 21¼, 22½)"

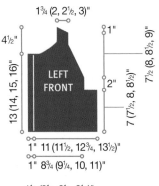

1¾ (2, 2½, 3)"
4½"
1"
7½ (8, 8½, 9)"
13 (14, 15, 16)"
2"
7 (7½, 8, 8½)"
LEFT FRONT
1" 11 (11½, 12¾, 13½)"
1" 8¾ (9¼, 10, 11)"

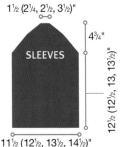

1½ (2¼, 2½, 3½)"
4¾"
12½ (12½, 13, 13½)"
SLEEVES
11½ (12½, 13½, 14½)"

Rose Callahan

7 (7½, 8, 8½)"/17.5 (19, 20.5, 21.5) cm from beg, end with a WS row. **Next (dec) row** [P1, k1] 3 times, k11 (12, 13, 15) sts, [k2tog] 10 (10, 12, 12) times, k17 (18, 19, 21) sts—44 (46, 50, 54) sts. Cont to work as established until piece measures same as back to armhole, shape armhole at side edge only as for back. AT THE SAME TIME, when armhole measures 4 (4½, 5, 5½)"/10 (11.5, 12.5, 14)cm, end with a WS row.

Shape neck and shoulder
Next row (RS) Bind off 8 (9, 9, 10) sts, work to end. Cont to bind off 3 sts from neck edge twice, then 2 sts twice.
Dec row (RS) K1, k2tog, work to end. Rep dec row every other row 4 times more. Work until same length as back to shoulder. Shape shoulder at side edge as for back.

SLEEVES
With larger needle and A, cast on 52 (56, 60, 66) sts. Change to smaller needles and MC. Work in k1, p1 rib for 2 rows. Cont in St st and work even until piece measures 12½ (12½, 13, 13½)"/31.5 (31.5, 33, 34)cm from beg, end with a WS row.

Shape cap
Dec row 1 (RS) K1, k2tog, k to last 3 sts, ssk, k1. Purl next row. Rep last 2 rows 10 times more, then dec row 1 once—28 (32, 36, 42) sts.
Dec row 2 (WS) P1, p2tog tbl, p to last 3 sts, p2tog, p1. Rep dec rows 1 and 2 four times more—10 (14, 18, 24) sts. Bind off 2 (2, 3, 4) sts at beg of next 2 rows. Bind off rem 6 (10, 12, 16) sts.

FINISHING
Block pieces to measurements. Sew shoulder seams. Set in sleeves. Sew side and sleeve seams.

Neckband
With larger needle and A, cast on 118 (118, 122, 122) sts. Change to smaller needles and MC. Work in k1, p1 rib for 8 rows. Bind off loosely in rib. Sew bound-off edge of neckband to neck edge.

FLOWER PIN
Small petals (make 3)
With crochet hook and MC, ch 4.
Row 1 Sc in 2nd ch from hook and in each ch across—3 sts. Ch 1, turn. **Row 2** Work 2 sc in first st, sc in next st, work 2 sc in last st—5 sts. Ch 1, turn. **Row 3** Work 2 sc in first st, sc in next 3 sts, work 2 sc in last st—7 sts. Ch 1, turn.
Row 4 Sc in each st across. Ch 1, turn.
Row 5 Sc in first st, skip next st, sc in next 3 sts, skip next st, sc in last st—5 sts. Ch 1, turn. **Row 6** Sc in first st, skip next st, sc in next st, skip next st, sc in last st—3 sts. Fasten off.

Medium petals (make 3)
With crochet hook and A, ch 5.
Row 1 Sc in 2nd ch from hook and in each ch across—4 sts. Ch 1, turn.
Row 2 Work 2 sc in first st, sc in next 2 sts, work 2 sc in last st—6 sts. Ch 1, turn.
Row 3 Work 2 sc in first st, sc in next 4 sts, work 2 sc in last st—8 sts. Ch 1, turn.
Rows 4 and 5 Sc in each st across. Ch 1,

turn. **Row 6** Sc in first st, skip next st, sc in next 4 sts, skip next st, sc in last st—6 sts. Ch 1, turn. **Row 7** Sc in first st, skip next st, sc in next 2 sts, skip next st, sc in last st—4 sts. Fasten off.

Large petals (make 3)
With crochet hook and A, ch 7.
Row 1 Sc in 2nd ch from hook and in each ch across—6 sts. Ch 1, turn.
Row 2 Work 2 sc in first st, sc in next 4 sts, work 2 sc in last st—8 sts. Ch 1, turn.
Row 3 Work 2 sc in first st, sc in next 6 sts, work 2 sc in last st—10 sts. Ch 1, turn. **Rows 4–7** Sc in each st across. Ch 1, turn. **Row 8** Sc in first st, skip next st, sc in next 6 sts, skip next st, sc in last st—8 sts. Ch 1, turn. **Row 9** Sc in first st, skip next st, sc in next 4 sts, skip next st, sc in last st—6 sts. Fasten off.

Leaves (make 3)
With crochet hook and B, ch 10.
Rnd 1 Sc in 2nd ch from hook and in next 8 ch, ch 1, turn to bottom loops of ch, sc in next 9 loops, ch 1, join rnd with a sl st in first st. **Rnd 2** Ch 1, sc in first 9 sts, ch 3, sc in each st to end, ch 3, join rnd with a sl st in first st. Fasten off.

Stem
With crochet hook and A, ch 74.
Row 1 Sl st in 2nd ch from hook, sl st in next 4 ch, [work (sl st, ch 3, sl st) in next ch (picot made), sl st in next 16 ch] twice, [work (sl st, ch 3, sl st) in next ch, sl st in next 10 ch] 3 times. Fasten off.

FINISHING
Use matching sewing threads throughout. Sew bottom edges of small petals tog, overlapping side edges slightly. Rep for medium and large petals. Place medium petals on top of large petals so medium petals are positioned between the large petals; tack tog at center. Place small petals on top of medium petals so small petals are positioned between the medium petals; sew all three layers tog at center. Sew on pin back. Fold stem so ends are uneven. Sew fold just below pin back. Sew leaves onto stem as shown.

SHORT sleeve top

Rose Callahan

SIZES
Sized for X-Small, Small, Medium. Shown in size Small.

KNITTED MEASUREMENTS
Bust 33 (37, 40)"/83.5 (94, 101.5)cm
Length 18 (19, 20)"/45.5 (48.5, 50.5)cm
Upper arm 16 (17, 18)"/40.5 (43, 45.5)cm

GAUGE
22 sts and 29 rows to 4"/10cm over St st using larger needles.
Take time to check gauge.

STITCH GLOSSARY
Picot point edging
(To bind off a multiple of 4 sts plus 2)

Bind off 2 sts, *sl rem st on RH needle to LH needle, cable cast on 2 sts, bind off 5 sts; rep from * to end. Fasten off rem st.

BACK
With larger needles, cast on 90 (102, 110) sts. **Row 1 (RS)** P2, *k2, p2; rep from * to end. **Row 2** K the knit sts and p the purl sts. Rep rows 1 and 2 for k2, p2 rib until piece measures 6½"/16.5cm from beg (48 rows). Change to St st and work even until piece measures 10 (10½, 11)"/25.5 (26.5, 28)cm from beg, end with a WS row.

Shape raglan armhole
Bind off 6 (6, 7) sts at beg of next 2 rows—78 (90, 96) sts.
Dec row (RS) K1, ssk,yo, ssk, k to last 5 sts, k2tog, yo, k2tog, k1. **Next row** P1,

k1, p to last 2 sts, k1, p1. Rep last 2 rows 23 (25, 27) times more. Bind off rem 30 (38, 40) sts.

FRONT
With larger needles, cast on 90 (102, 110) sts.

Beg chart
Row 1 (RS) Beg as indicated work to end of chart for chosen size (center of piece), work chart backwards from center (from left to right), end as indicated. Cont in

You'll Need

For Sweater
YARN ③
- 13¹/₅oz/375g(13¹/₅oz/375g, 17½oz/500g) or 750yd/690m (750yd/690m, 1000yd/920m) of any DK weight cotton

NEEDLES
- One pair each sizes 5 and 6 (3.75 and 4mm) needles *or size to obtain gauge*
- Size 5 (3.75mm) circular needle 16"/40cm

For Flower
YARN ①
- 1¾oz/50g or 200yd/180m of any fingering weight cotton yarn
- Small amount of sweater yarn for French knot centers

OTHER MATERIALS
- Size B-1 (2.25mm) crochet hook
- Two small safety pins
- White glue
- Small paintbrush or toothbrush

pat as established until all chart rows have been worked—piece measures 6½"/16.5cm from beg. Change to St st and work even until piece measures same length as back to armhole.

Shape raglan armhole
Work as for back until there are 48 (58, 60) sts.

Shape neck
Next row (RS) Work armhole dec, k10 (13, 13), join 2nd ball of yarn and bind off center 18 (22, 24) sts, work to last 5 sts, work armhole dec. **Next row** Work to last 2 sts on first half, p2tog; on 2nd half, p2tog, work to end. **Next row** Work armhole dec, work to last 3 sts on first half, k3tog; on 2nd half, k3tog, work to last 5 sts, work armhole dec. Rep last 2 rows twice more—2 (5, 5) sts each side. **For size X-small only** Dec 1 st at each neck edge on next row. Fasten off.
For size Small and Medium only Dec 1 st at each neck edge on next row. Dec 1 st each armhole and neck edge on next row. K2tog each side and fasten off.

LEFT SLEEVE
With larger needles, cast on 88 (94, 100) sts. K 4 rows. Cont in St st for 2 rows.

Shape raglan cap
Bind off 6 (6, 7) sts at beg of next 2 rows—76 (82, 88) sts. Work dec row as for back raglan every RS row 6 (8, 10) times—64 (66, 66) sts. Mark the center 6 sts and work central decs as foll: **Center dec row (RS)** Work armhole dec, work to center 6 sts, ssk, k2, k2tog, work to last 5 sts, work armhole dec. Work 5 rows with armhole decs only. Rep center dec row. Rep last 6 rows 3 times more—26 (28, 30) sts. **Next row (WS)** Bind off 15 sts (neck edge), work to end—13

(15, 15) sts. Cont to work armhole decs and dec 1 st at neck edge every other row until 1 st rem. Fasten off.

RIGHT SLEEVE
Work to correspond to left sleeve, reversing shaping at top of sleeve cap.

FINISHING
Block pieces to measurements.

Sleeve edging
With WS facing and smaller needles, pick up and k 86 (94, 98) sts along lower

edge of each sleeve. Work picot point edging to bind off.
Sew raglan sleeve caps to raglan armholes.

Neck edging
With RS facing and circular needle, beg at left back shoulder seam, pick up and k 21 (23, 26) sts along top of left sleeve, 10 (12, 13) sts along left front neck edge, 18 (22, 26) sts along center front neck, 10 (12, 13) sts along right front neck, 21 (23, 26) sts along right sleeve and 30 (38, 42) sts along back neck—110 (130,

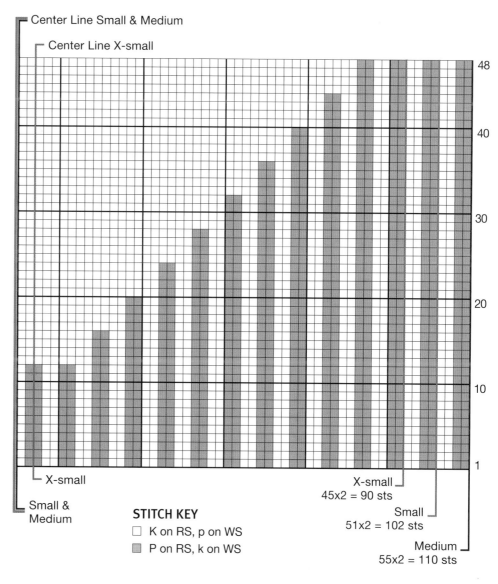

Center Line Small & Medium

Center Line X-small

X-small

Small & Medium

X-small
45x2 = 90 sts

Small
51x2 = 102 sts

Medium
55x2 = 110 sts

STITCH KEY
☐ K on RS, p on WS
▨ P on RS, k on WS

148) sts. P next rnd, dec 4 (4, 6) sts evenly across back neck—106 (126, 142) sts. K 1 rnd, p 1 rnd. Work picot point edging to bind off.
Sew side seams.

FLOWER

Note Flower consists of three petal layers: large, medium and small.

Large (6 petals)
Center
Ch 6. Join with sl st to first ch to form ring.
Rnd 1 Work 12 sc in ring. Ch 1.
Rnd 2 [2 sc in next sc, 1 sc in next sc] 6 times—18 sc. Ch 1.
Rnd 3 [2 sc in next sc, 1 sc in next 2 sc] 6 times—24 sc. Ch 1.
Rnd 4 [2 sc in next sc, 1 sc in next 3 sc] 6 times—30 sc. Ch 1.
Rnd 5 [2 sc in next sc, 1 sc in next 4 sc] 6 times—36 sc. Ch 1.

Petals
Row 1 Sc in next 6 sc. Ch 1, turn.
Rows 2–5 Rep row 1.
Row 6 Dec 1 sc, sc in next 2 sts, dec 1 sc. Fasten off.
Rep rows 1–6 five times more for a total of 6 petals.

Medium (5 petals)
Center
Ch 5. Join with sl st to first ch to form ring. **Rnd 1** Work 10 sc in ring. Ch 1.
Rnd 2 [2 sc in next sc, 1 sc in next sc] 5 times—15 sc. Ch 1. **Rnd 3** [2 sc in next sc, 1 sc in next 2 sc] 5 times—20 sc. Ch 1. **Rnd 4** [2 sc in next sc, 1 sc in next 3 sc] 5 times—25 sc. Ch 1.

Petals
Row 1 Sc in next 5 sc. Ch 1, turn.
Rows 2–3 Rep row 1. **Row 4** Dec 1 sc, sc in next sc, dec 1 sc. Fasten off.
Rep rows 1–4 three times more.
5th petal Work rows 1–3.
Row 4 Dec 1 sc, sc in next sc, dec 1 sc, using last st worked and next st

and fasten off tog.

Small (4 petals)
Center
Ch 4. Join with sl st to first ch to form ring.
Rnd 1 Work 8 sc in ring. Ch 1. **Rnd 2** Sc in each sc.
Rnd 3 2 sc in each sc—16 sc.

Petals
Row 1 Sc in next 4 sc. Ch 1, turn.
Row 2 Rep row 1.
Row 3 Dec 1 sc, dec 1 sc, using last st worked and next st and fasten off tog.
Rep rows 1–3 three times more for a total of 4 petals.

To stiffen and shape petals
(Do this on a clean surface where you can leave the petals until they dry) Using a small paint or toothbrush, brush the petals with a dilute mixture of white glue and water. Gently round the petals up so they look natural, and support them on the outside with small objects like pencils to hold them in position. Allow to dry. Place medium layer on top of large layer and small layer on top. Rotate them until the petals look natural and slightly off center. Tack them tog using a needle and white thread. Take a strand of the body cotton, and remove one or two of the plies to make it thinner. Using an embroidery needle and this strand, work a circle of 8 French knots around the center of the top petal layer. Pin flower to center front of garment.

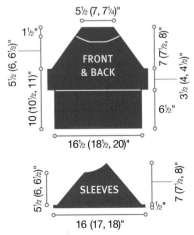

5½ (7, 7¼)"
1½"
5½ (6, 6½)"
10 (10½, 11)"
7 (7½, 8)"
3½ (4, 4½)"
6½"
16½ (18½, 20)"
FRONT & BACK

5½ (6, 6½)"
SLEEVES
7 (7½, 8)"
8½"
16 (17, 18)"